COUNTRY STYLE

HOME ACCESSORIES

HOME
ACCESSORIES

WARD LOCK

A WARD LOCK BOOK

First published in the UK 1995 by Ward Lock,
Wellington House, 125 Strand, London WC2R 0BB.

A Cassell Imprint

Copyright © Eaglemoss Publications Limited 1995
Based on The Country Look

Front cover pictures: EWA/Di Lewis (top left), Eaglemoss/John Suett (top right and bottom left), Ariadne (bottom right). Back cover picture: Eaglemoss/Simon Page Ritchie.

A British Library Cataloguing in Publication Data block for this book may be obtained from the British Library

ISBN 0 7063 7382 0
Printed and bound in Hong Kong

CONTENTS

Napkin finishes

A set of stylish napkins in bright and cheerful colours adds à flourish to any meal and invigorates existing table linen. Napkins with a dash of spring colours like primrose yellow or violet are great for summer picnics in the garden or out in a park, and in autumnal reds and greens or elegant dusky shades, they have a formal look which is ideal for dinner parties.

If the table decorations need sparkle, or you just feel like a change, decorative table napkins are an economical way of introducing a fresh new look. It isn't even necessary to make new napkins – just give the existing set new vigour with a coloured binding, a row of stitching or a trimming. If the tablecloth is in good order, a similar trimming can be added,

and the whole set will look like new.

There are, however, times when you will want to make new napkins and have a completely fresh start. Pick a colour from the tablecloth – not necessarily the main colour – and repeat it in the napkin fabric or its trimmings. If there are several co-ordinating fabrics which take your fancy, mix and match them to give the set extra spice.

Any soft but durable, woven fabric can be used for the table napkins, but for best results the main fabric should look good on both sides. Cotton and linen are lovely and look crisp and fresh when pressed, but a synthetic mix will be easier to clean. For fringing, a loose-weave fabric is better to work with as the threads come away easily.

▲ Fabulous fringing
Fringing is one of the easiest finishes to give a napkin you have made yourself, and it's also one of the nicest. Its simplicity means that it goes well in most settings.

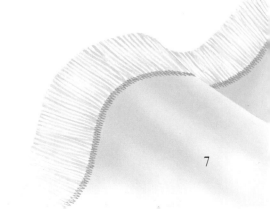

FRINGING

A fringed edge is an attractive finish for even-weave fabrics such as linen or linen-look fabric. It works particularly well with striped or checked patterns.

1 Cutting out Cut out a fabric square for each napkin to the finished size – 50 × 50cm (20 × 20in) for a large napkin.

2 Making the fringe Decide on the finished depth of the fringe and mark a line this depth from the edge all round. Stitch along the marked line with a close zigzag. Cut to the stitching at 6cm (2½in) intervals all round, then use a pin to pull away the horizontal threads in between to make the fringe.

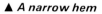

▲ *A narrow hem*

NARROW HEM

A narrow hem is a subtle, and very simple finish for a new napkin. It works well on elegant or bold fabrics which do not require the additional decorative interest of a trimming.

1 Cutting out Cut a square of fabric 50 × 50cm (20 × 20in) for each of the napkins – six napkins can be made from 1.6m (1⅞yd) of 120cm (48in) wide fabric.

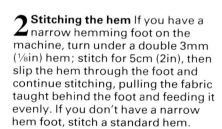

2 Stitching the hem If you have a narrow hemming foot on the machine, turn under a double 3mm (⅛in) hem; stitch for 5cm (2in), then slip the hem through the foot and continue stitching, pulling the fabric taught behind the foot and feeding it evenly. If you don't have a narrow hem foot, stitch a standard hem.

▼ *Wide hem with ribbon trim*

WIDE HEM

This is a very elegant finish for fine napkins. The wide hem is mitred at the corners and the raw edges are covered with satin ribbon or a row of decorative satin stitch.

1 Cutting out Cut out a piece of fabric for each napkin, adding the depth of the hem all round.

2 Hemming the napkins Turn the hem to the right side of the napkin and pin. Fold under the excess fabric at the corners to mitre. Pin and stitch over the raw edge of the hem with wide, close zigzag. Alternatively, pin ribbon over the raw edge of the hem, folding at the corners in line with the fabric mitres. Pin and then topstitch along each long edge of the ribbon to finish.

◀ *Wide hem with zigzag*

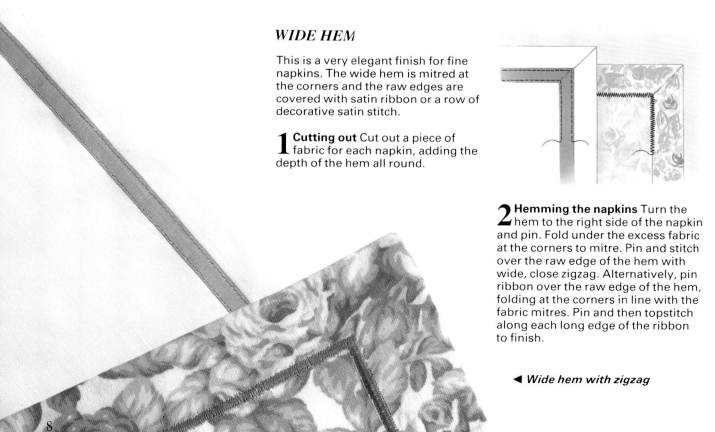

▲ Stitching link

A wide hem with machine zigzag gives this napkin an attractive finish. The machine stitching brings out the pink in the fabric and links the napkin in more closely with the plates.

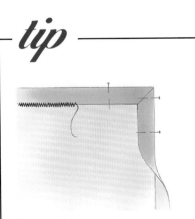

tip

Reversible napkin

If your favourite fabrics have a definite right and wrong side, you can still choose them for hemmed or bound napkins by using two together. Cut out two pieces of fabric the finished size, adding the depth of the hem to one piece for the hemmed napkin. Pin them wrong sides together. Bind the edges or turn up the hem and finish with close zigzag or ribbon.

BINDING

A binding trim gives plain napkins a fresh and colourful finish. It can be added to ready-made napkins to co-ordinate them with a new tablecloth or tablemats, or used to give a decorative finish to napkins you have made yourself. Use ready-made bias binding for quick results, or make your own from a strip of co-ordinating fabric.

1 Cutting out Cut out the fabric for each napkin to the finished size. Measure round the fabric and cut a strip of the binding fabric to that measurement, adding 2cm (¾in) for the join. The binding should be twice the finished width plus 1cm (½in).

▼ Bound hem

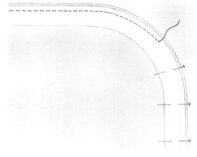

2 Binding the napkin If using a ready-made napkin, unpick or trim off the old hem first. Pin the binding to one edge of the napkin with right sides facing, and mark and then stitch a mitre at the corner (see page 12). Continue all the way round, joining the ends at a corner by stitching in a mitre. Stitch to the napkin, 5mm (¼in) from the raw edge, then turn the binding to the other side and slipstitch in place.

◄ *Lace edging*

LACE CORNERS

Lace motifs can be added to one or two corners of each napkin for a subtle but attractive effect. Throw a length of lacy fabric over an existing tablecloth to give the room a co-ordinated look.

1 Cutting out Cut out the napkin and stitch a narrow hem all round. Cut a piece of fusible webbing the same size as the motif and iron on to the back of the lace.

2 Applying the lace Fuse the lace to a corner of the napkin with a warm iron. To ensure the motif is secure, stitch round the inside edge of the motif using a narrow, close zigzag. Trim the napkin fabric just beyond the stitching if required.

LACE EDGING

A touch of lace on a napkin gives it a delicate look which is ideal for special occasions. Add to a ready-made napkin to give it that little bit extra, or use to enliven a home-made napkin in a plain or subtly patterned fabric.

1 Cutting out Cut out a piece of fabric for each napkin the finished size plus 1cm (⅜in) all round. Cut out enough lace to go round the edge, adding 2cm (¾in) for the join.

◄ *Lace motif*

2 Stitching the napkin Turn the 1cm (⅜in) hem allowance, mitring the corners; tack. Pin the lace on top with the inner edge just overlapping the raw edge of the fabric; trim the fabric a little if necessary to do this. Topstitch through all layers on each side of the raw hem to neaten and prevent fraying.

◄ *Lovely lace*
A lace trimming gives this napkin a fresh and elegant finish which is ideal for parties and special events.

Quilted tablemats

T able linen is the crowning glory of the dinner table, setting the style of the meal, and helping to create atmosphere. At breakfast, table linen in bright colours is fresh and cheering, while for dinner something in a deep, rich pattern or in traditional white damask sets a formal tone.

Fabric selection

When choosing fabrics for the table, consider both the setting and the colour scheme. If the table is in the kitchen, meals on it are likely to be informal, so choose your pattern accordingly. Make sure the pattern is small enough to suit the size of the placemat, and to enable you to use the fabric economically. With larger patterns you may need extra fabric to make a set of identical mats.

Plain white or cream fabrics make beautiful napkins and placemats, but they show the stains. Reserve these for dinner parties, and choose a small, overall pattern for everyday use. Synthetics are easiest to care for, so consider using polyester cotton which is both strong and easy to clean.

▲ **French country style**
The mini-print designs of Provençal fabrics are ideal for table linen; the bright colours bring the warmth of the Mediterranean sun to the table, setting a relaxed, holiday atmosphere.

Materials

For a set of six bordered tablemats you will need 1.2m (1 ⅜yd) of 120cm (48in) wide **furnishing fabric** for the main pieces, plus a 10m (10½yd) strip for the border.

For six quilted mats you will need 1.4m (1½yd) of 120cm (48in) wide **furnishing fabric** plus the same of 100cm (36in) wide **lightweight wadding (batting)**. You will also need 10m (10½yd) of **bias binding**. You can make six napkins from 1.6m (1⅞yd) of 120cm (48in) wide **fabric**.

BORDERED PLACEMATS

1 Cutting out From the main fabric cut a piece of fabric 2cm (¾in) longer and wider than the required finished size. Two common finished sizes are 45 x 30cm (17¾ x 11¾in) and 40 x 35cm (15¾ x 13¾in). Choose the shape you prefer, but make sure the mat can take a complete plate setting.

For the border you will need fabric strips 8-10cm (3-4in) wide depending on the pattern and effect you want. Cut two strips the width of the finished mat plus 2cm (¾in) long, and two strips the length of the finished mat plus 2cm (¾in) long.

2 Press seam allowances Press a 1cm (⅜in) seam allowance to the right side all the way round the main piece. Press under 5mm (¼in) along the long edges of all the strips.

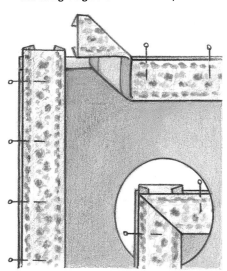

3 Pinning mitres Take one of the two longer strips of fabric and place it 1cm (⅜in) beyond the end of the mat, with one side edge level with the folded edge of the mat; pin. Take one short strip and place it in the same way along the edge at right angles to the first strip. Tuck the end under so it is level with the end of the first strip; press and pin. Repeat to pin mitres round the placemat to form a frame.

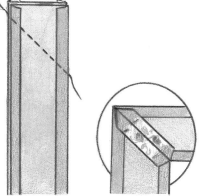

▲ **Raspberry border**
A pretty fabric border with a fruity theme is the crowning glory of this simple, but effective placemat.

▼ **Green dream**
Green and white is a fresh and cool combination for the table.

4 Stitching the border Mark the diagonal lines of the border mitres with tailor's chalk. Remove the pins, and with right sides facing pin and then stitch the border, using the chalk lines as a stitching guide. Check the fit on the placemat; trim away the excess seam allowance.

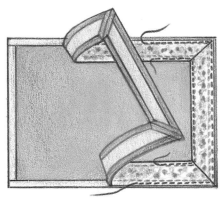

5 Completing the mat Pin the frame of fabric to the mat, with seam allowances enclosed. Tack or pin in place, then machine stitch close to both edges of the border frame, pivoting at corners.

QUILTED OVAL PLACEMAT

1 Cutting out For each mat cut out two pieces of fabric and one piece of wadding to the required finished size (see bordered mat, step 1). Alternatively cut one piece of ready-quilted fabric to this measurement. You will also need 1.6m (1⅝yd) bias binding.

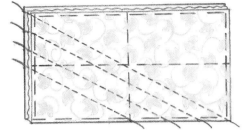

2 Quilting the fabric Unless using ready-quilted fabric, sandwich the wadding between the wrong sides of the two fabric pieces. Tack together round the edge and in a cross across the middle to prevent the wadding from slipping while you stitch. Draw a diagonal chalk line between opposite corners of the mat. Stitch along the line and then in rows up to 3cm (1¼in) away to form channels. Use a quilting bar for accuracy. Draw a line between the other two corners of the mat and stitch in the same way to make a diamond pattern. Remove tacking stitches.

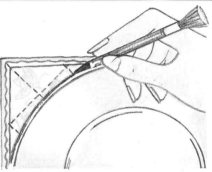

3 Shaping the mat Place a bowl or plate in each corner of the mat and draw round it with tailor's chalk. Cut along the chalk line.

4 Binding the edges Stitch the mat 5mm (¼in) from the edge all round, and trim wadding close to the stitching to reduce bulk. Using the mat as a guide, steam iron the binding into a curve at the corners. Carefully stitch the bias binding to the edge of the mat to finish the raw edges.

tip

Reversible mats
By using two different fabrics for the bound and quilted placemats, you can make the mats reversible. Choose fabrics which are different in style and colour for a total contrast, and bind the edges in a colour which goes with both of the fabrics used.

▲ Colour match
Pick out colours from your china when choosing the tablemat fabrics, to achieve a really attractive setting.

RECTANGULAR PLACEMAT

1 Quilting the fabric Cut and quilt the fabric as in steps 1 and 2 for the oval mat. Stitch the mat all round 5mm (¼in) from the edge; trim the wadding close to the stitching.

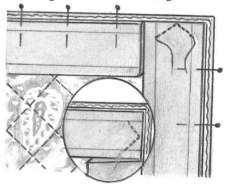

2 Stitching corners Pin the unfolded binding along one edge of the mat, with stitching lines matching. At the corner, fold the binding under, then turn each corner down to the centre fold and finger press. Open out the binding and stitch along the diagonal pressed lines between the stitching lines. Continue round the mat, joining the ends of the binding together at a corner by stitching in a mitre.

3 Attaching the binding Tack and then stitch the binding to the mat; remove the tacking. Turn the binding to the wrong side of the fabric and then slipstitch in place.

FRILLED PLACEMAT

1 Making the mat Cut out the fabric and wadding for the mat, then quilt and shape as for the oval mat steps 1, 2 and 3. Since the frill will add to the size of the mat, make this 4cm (1⅝in) smaller all round than the required finished size. Neaten the raw edges with zigzag, overlock or narrow bias binding.

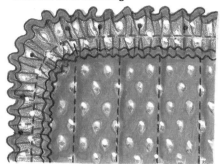

Making a bound frill For a frill bound on both edges, cut out and join strips of fabric 5cm (2in) wide to make up a strip 1½-2 times the measurement round the mat. Join into a ring and bind both edges. Run a row of gathering stitches 2cm (¾in) from one edge, and pull up to fit the stitching line of the mat. Pin, tack and then stitch close to the gathering threads; remove tacking.

Making a hemmed frill For a simple hemmed frill, cut out and join strips of fabric 9cm (3½in) wide. Join into a ring and make a double 1cm (⅜in) hem along both edges. Stitch a row of gathering stitches 2cm (¾in) from one edge and pull up to fit the stitching line of the mat. Tack then stitch close to the gathering threads; remove tacking.

▲ Patterned pair
Using one pattern in two colourways makes these two fabrics go together, and the red binding on the frill ensures that the pairing is complete. This idea would also work well for making reversible quilted placemats.

◄ Neat napkin
Mitred corners give a neat finish to plain napkins. Keep the mitres flat with a few stitches made when sewing the hems.

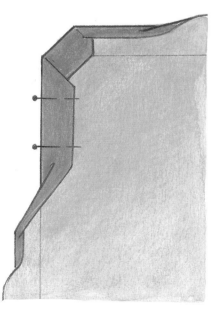

SIMPLE NAPKIN

1 Cutting and pressing For a finished napkin 50cm (20in) square, cut a piece of fabric 53cm (21¾in) square. On all edges, turn 1.5cm (⅝in) to the wrong side and press; unfold. Fold each corner over in a triangle, so the foldlines still line up. Fold the triangle in half by folding back the tip of the triangle to the first fold; trim off the tip as shown right.

2 Making the hems Fold the raw edges over by 5mm (¼in) and press. Fold again along the crease to hem the fabric. Pin or tack and then hem with small slipstitches.

Stylish stripes for tables

A clever choice of table linen can transform a plain dinner table into a really stylish setting, and is essential when it comes to creating atmosphere. Freshness, vitality and hints of early spring are the messages given out by the stunning green and white striped set pictured here. Use it to brighten up family mealtimes, or to set the scene for an informal dinner with friends.

The table linen is made from striped and plain fabrics in only two colours – a strong, fresh green and crisp white. By combining the fabrics and colours in different ways, you can create a whole range of individual, but perfectly co-ordinated table accessories. For example, the placemats (shown overleaf) are made from striped fabric, trimmed with a green border, while the napkins are plain white with eye-catching green appliqué details and a stripy frill.

Like the napkins, the fitted table-cloth has an attractively frilled edge, which combines well with the straight lines of the striped fabric, as do the

▲ Go for green
Combine a lively green and white striped fabric with crisp plain cottons in matching colours, to create a brilliant set of table linen. It's ideal for informal lunches or summer dinners.

curves of the placemats' scalloped borders. Use a strong cotton fabric to make the table linen, or a synthetic mix which will look just as good and be easier to clean.

Materials

Green and white striped fabric for the tablecloth, the frilled napkin trimming, the placemats and the cutlery ties; see individual instructions for quantities

Plain green fabric to trim the placemats and to make matching cutlery ties; you will need about 1m (40in) squared to make six mats and several ties

Plain white fabric to make the napkins; you will need about 130 x 90cm (51 x 35in) to make six napkins

Pale green Funtex for the appliquéd napkin motifs; this is a fine, washable felt-like fabric, available from most department stores and haberdashery shops

Fusible webbing (Bondaweb) to fix the motifs and the placemat borders

Dark green fabric paint or **pen**

Stiff card to make a template for the placemat borders

Matching sewing threads

Sharp scissors

Tailor's chalk

FITTED TABLECLOTH

The instructions given here are for a frilled rectangular tablecloth, but can be easily adapted to make a circular one.

1 Measuring up For the top panel, measure the width and length of the table, and add 1.5cm (⅝in) all round for seam allowances. Decide how long you would like the frilled sides of the tablecloth to be – a mid-length drop of 40-60cm (16-24in) is often best for a kitchen or dining table; add 3.5cm (1⅜in) to this measurement. The width of the frill is one and a half to twice the measurement around the table-top.

2 Cutting out Cut out the top panel to the correct dimensions, with the stripes on the fabric lying lengthways; join fabric widths if necessary, matching the pattern and avoiding a central seam. To gain the required width for the frill, you will need to cut out and join fabric widths. Cut as many as are needed to make up the correct width, allowing a little extra for side seams. The stripes on the frill lie lengthways.

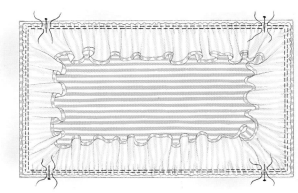

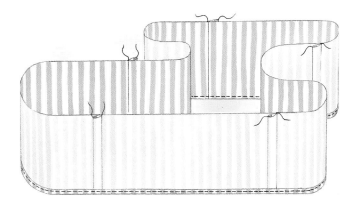

3 Joining the frill sections Use French seams to join together the fabric widths for the frill; then join the two ends of the long strip to create a ring of fabric. Pin and stitch a double 1cm (⅜in) hem along the bottom edge of the frill.

▶ All tied up
Cutlery ties in co-ordinated striped or plain fabrics add the finishing touch to this set, and can be easily made from leftover scraps of fabric.

4 Gathering up the frill Divide the top panel and the long raw edge of the frill into four equal sections, marking each one at the fabric edge with tailor's chalk. Run two rows of gathering threads along the raw edge of the frill, 1cm (⅜in) and then 2cm (¾in) in from the edge, stopping and starting at the chalk marks. With right sides together, match up the chalk marks on the top panel and the frill, and pin together over each mark. Pull on the threads until each section fits panel.

5 Attaching the frill Pin, tack and stitch the top panel and the frill together, taking a 1.5cm (⅝in) seam allowance. Neaten raw edges and press to finish.

◀ *Curves and stripes*
The scalloped border on these stripy placemats gives their outline definition when set against the tablecloth, and softens the overall lined effect. When not in use, simply roll the mats up and secure them with easy to make matching fabric ties.
To introduce a little variety into the set, make a few mats in the plain green or white fabric, and use the striped fabric as the border material.

BORDERED PLACEMATS

The placemats are made from the same striped fabric as the tablecloth, but have a decorative scalloped border in plain green. Rather than making a border from fabric strips with mitred corners, the border is cut out in one piece from a rectangle of fabric; the leftover green fabric from the centre can then be used to make cutlery or napkin ties.

1 Cutting out For each placemat, cut one rectangle of plain green fabric, 47 x 32cm (18½ x 12½in), and two of striped fabric to the same size, with the stripes lying along the short edge.

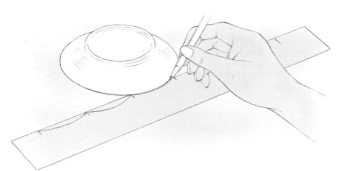

2 Making a border template Make a scalloped card template for shaping the border. Cut a strip of stiff card, 47 x 4.5cm (18½ x 1¾in). Mark off 4.5cm (1¾in) at each short end of the strip, then divide the middle section into five equal parts of about 7.5cm (3in), marking off each one at the card's long edge. Using a cup or saucer as a guide, join the pencil marks with a curve, to create a line of five scallops. Cut along the scalloped line to make the template.

Making cutlery ties
Cut fabric strips, and fold them in half lengthways with right sides together. Stitch down side and one end; turn to right side and slipstitch to close.

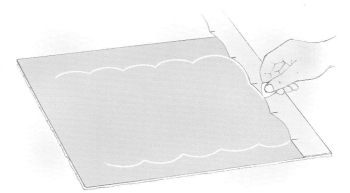

3 Transferring the border Apply Bondaweb to the wrong side of the green border fabric, around the edges only. Place template over one long edge of the rectangle. Draw around the template edge with tailor's chalk to transfer the border on to the fabric; the last scallop tip at each end will lie 4.5cm (1¾in) in from fabric edge. Repeat on other long edge. Place template over each short edge, and trace off three scallops, starting and ending 4.5cm (1¾in) in from the edge.

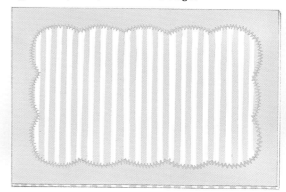

4 Cutting and stitching the border Cut out the border, following the curved edges of the scallops, then remove the Bondaweb backing. With edges matching, place the border over the right side of one of the striped fabric rectangles, and iron in place. Use matching green thread to zigzag stitch along the scalloped edge of the border, to neaten the edge and firmly secure.

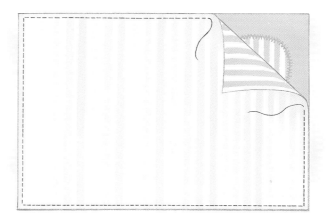

5 Making up the mat With edges matching and right sides together, place the second striped fabric rectangle on top of the first, enclosing the border. Stitch around the edges, taking a 1cm (⅜in) seam allowance and leaving a small opening in one side. Turn through to right side and slipstitch the opening closed. Topstitch around outer edges of border to help the mat lie flat.

17

APPLIQUÉ NAPKINS

1 Cutting out For each napkin, cut a square of white fabric measuring 42cm (16½in). For the frilled trimming, cut widths from the striped fabric, 15cm (6in) deep, and stitch together until you have a single strip 2.5m (98in) long – ie 1½ times the circumference of the napkin.

2 Attaching the frill With right sides facing, fold the fabric strip in half, and stitch along edge to form a tube. Turn through to right side and press, then stitch the ends together. Run two rows of gathering threads along the pressed edge of the strip, 5mm (¼in) and 1.5cm (⅝in) in from edge. Gather up the frill and stitch it to the napkin edge, taking a 1cm (⅜in) seam allowance. Trim the raw edges of the napkin, then topstitch it to the frill, enclosing raw edges.

▼ Cool as a cucumber
To give each napkin a personal touch, appliqué a different fruit or vegetable motif to each one. With a green fabric pen, you can also fill in decorative detail, as on the cucumber slice shown here.

3 Preparing the appliqué motifs On stiff card, draw then cut out templates for the appliqué motifs, for example a slice of cucumber, an apple and celery leaves, as shown here. Iron a piece of Bondaweb to one side of the pale green Funtex, then draw round your templates to transfer the motifs on to the Funtex. Cut out.

4 Applying the motifs Remove the Bondaweb backing and position a motif in one corner of each napkin. Iron the motif in place. To hold it firmly in position, use a matching thread to zigzag stitch around the motif edges. To add detail to the cucumber motif, use a dark green fabric pen to draw in its seeds and skin.

Quilted tea set

Make this pretty tea set from oddments of furnishing fabric to match the colour scheme of your room or your tea service. The table runner and tea-cosy are lightly quilted keeping the pot warm and preventing it making heat marks on the table. The size given for the cosy is suitable for the average teapot, but use the paper pattern to check the fit before cutting out the fabric. Finish off the set with a matching holder for cakes or rolls.

If you use cotton fabrics and synthetic wadding the set can be washed from time to time to keep it fresh.

THE ROLL HOLDER

Materials

Printed glazed cotton 109 x 35cm (43 x 14in)
Plain glazed cotton 109 x 35cm (43 x 14in)
Bias binding 12mm wide x 3.4m (3³/₄ yds) to match printed cotton
Satin ribbon 5mm wide x 1.5m (1³/₄yds) to match bias binding
Sewing thread to match bias binding and plain glazed cotton
Embroidery needle size 7
Dressmaker's marking pencil

1 **Cutting out the fabric** Make a circular template 34cm (13½in) in diameter. Cut out three circles from the printed glazed cotton and three from the plain glazed cotton.

2 **Making the lower circle** Pin the wrong sides of two of the printed circles together and edge with the matching bias binding.

▼ *Tea time treats*
Mint green fabric with a pink trim adds freshness to the floral print.

3 **Making the middle circle** Trim 2cm (³/₄in) from edge all round a printed circle and a plain circle, then pin them together with wrong sides facing. Edge with the bias binding.

4 **Making the top circle** Using the remaining two plain circles, trim 2cm (³/₄in) from edge all round, then pin them together with wrong sides facing. Edge with the bias binding.

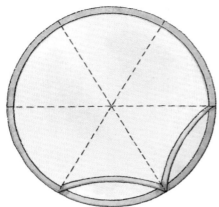

5 **Joining the top and middle circles** Fold the top circle into six segments and press to mark folds. Place the top circle on to the middle circle and pin the two layers together at the centre of each segment, then machine with a straight stitch along the folds to form pockets.

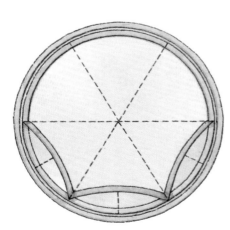

6 **Joining the middle and lower circles** Fold the lower circle into six segments and press to mark folds. Place the middle circle on to the lower circle and pin the two layers together with each fold of the lower circle at the centre of each middle segment. Stitch for about 7cm (2³/₄in) from the outer edge, along the folds, to form pockets.

7 **Attaching the ribbon ties** Cut the ribbon into six 25cm (10in) lengths and sew to the edge of the top circle at the centre of each pocket. Tie the ribbons opposite each other and make a bow.

THE TABLE RUNNER

Materials
Printed glazed cotton 80 x 45cm (31½ x 17 ³/₄in)
Cotton fabric for lining 80 x 45cm (31½ x 17 ³/₄in)
Lightweight synthetic wadding (batting) 90 x 55cm (35½ x 21¾in)
Bias binding 2.5cm (1 in) wide x 2.40m (2⁵/₈yd) one length in each of two contrasting colours to match printed cotton
Sewing thread to match plain fabric and contrast bias binding

Embroidery needle size 7
Quilting foot for sewing machine
Dressmaker's marking pencil
Tissue paper to cover an area of 90 x 55cm (35½ x 21³/₄in) for quilting

1 **Prepare the fabric for quilting** Fold the piece of printed cotton once widthways and once lengthways and press with an iron to divide the material into quarters. Open out and mark along the folds using the marking pencil.

2 Tacking the wadding

Place the wadding on the wrong side of the printed fabric leaving 5cm (2in) excess wadding all round. Place the tissue paper over the wadding and pin through all layers, smoothing out the layers from the centre. Tack through all layers along the marked lines from centre to outer edge, then tack a grid of 10cm (4in) squares over the fabric.

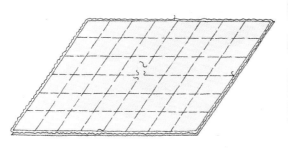

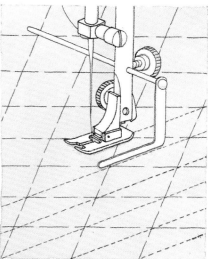

3 Quilting the fabric

Using the dressmaker's marking pencil and a ruler, mark a diagonal line across the fabric joining the corners of each square on the tacked grid. Using a long machine stitch and the quilting foot, machine along this line. Adjust the quilting foot guide-bar to a space of 4cm (1½in) and lining up the guide-bar with the previous stitching line, stitch lines across the fabric parallel to the first diagonal line.

Working in the opposite direction, stitch diagonal lines in the same way as before. Trim the wadding to the same size as the fabric and remove the tacking stitches and tissue paper.

4 Lining the table runner

With right sides of printed cotton and lining together, stitch a 1cm (³/₈in) seam around the edge, leaving a 15cm (6in) space in the seam. Snip across corners and turn right side out. Slipstitch the opening together and press.

5 Adding the binding trim

Beginning at one corner, and working mock mitred corners, pin one contrast coloured bias binding, 4cm (1½in) from the edge, around the runner and slipstitch into place along both edges.

Beginning at the same corner as before, and just overlapping the first contrast coloured bias binding, pin the second bias binding into place outside the first binding, mock mitring the corners. Slipstitch both edges, then press the runner.

◄ *Breakfast special*
Use the runner as a top cloth for the breakfast table. The appliqué teapot motif can be slightly padded to add a three dimensional effect.

MAKING THE TEA-COSY

Materials

Plain glazed cotton 90 x 55cm (35½ x 21¾in)

Printed glazed cotton 70 x 30cm (27½ x 12in)

Mediumweight synthetic wadding (batting) 55 x 90cm (21¾ x 35½in)

Cotton lining fabric 75 x 50cm (29½ x 19¾in) for lining

Bias binding 2.5cm (1in) wide x 1.40m (1½yd) to match printed fabric

Sewing thread to match plain glazed cotton

Embroidery needle size 7

Quilting foot for sewing machine

Dressmaker's marking pencil

Tissue paper to cover an area of 55 x 90cm (21¾ x 35½in) for quilting

1 **Cut out the fabric** Using the plain fabric instead of the printed fabric prepare and quilt the layers of fabric, wadding and tissue together, as given in steps 1 and 2 of the table runner.

2 **Make a pattern** Following the diagram, make a paper pattern for the tea-cosy, drawing the teapot design on to the pattern.

3 **Cut out the fabric** Cut out two tea-cosy shapes from the quilted fabric and two from the lining. Cut out the teapot design from the paper pattern and use it to cut out the teapot motif from the printed glazed cotton.

4 **Prepare the teapot motif** Taking care not to pull the motif out of shape, work a line of stitching 3mm (¼in) round the edge of motif. Snip into corners and around the curves to the stitching line. Turn a small 3mm (¼in) hem along the stitching to wrong side along shaped edges of teapot and press.

5 **Appliqué the motif** Matching the base of teapot motif with straight edge of cosy front, centre the motif and pin in place. Cut a 20cm (8in) length of bias binding and fold in half lengthways. Pin on to front for teapot handle, tucking the ends under motif. Slipstitch handle and teapot in place.

6 **Complete the appliqué** Cut a length of bias binding for teapot lid rim adding 6mm (¼in) extra each end. Fold 6mm (¼in) under at each end of the bias binding and press, then fold binding into three lengthways, press and stitch on to motif for lid rim. Cut a circle 2cm (¾in) in diameter from bias binding for teapot lid knob. Turn under a narrow hem, pad slightly with wadding, and stitch into place.

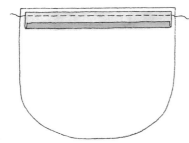

7 **Adding binding to lining** With one side of bias binding opened out, place raw edge of binding to right side of lining and stitch along crease.

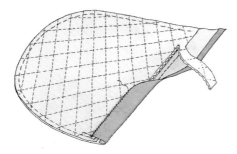

8 **Joining the lining and cosy** Trim 6mm (¼in) from lower edge of quilted fabric and place to lining wrong sides together. Tack round curved edge. Turn bias binding to quilted side and slipstitch along second folded edge. Repeat for other half of cosy.

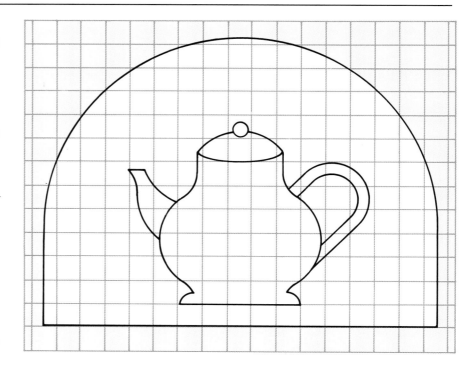

Chart for tea-cosy and appliqué Draw a grid of 2.5cm (1in) squares on a sheet of paper and transfer the shapes to make the pattern.

9 **Quilt the binding** Run a line of stitches along the centre of the binding on each piece.

10 **Making the tea-cosy** With lining of the tea-cosy back and front together, stitch a seam 1cm (⅜in) around curved edge.

11 **Make the printed bias binding** Cut bias strips 5cm (2in) wide from the printed fabric and join together until the strip is approximately 90cm (1yd) long (see page 93). Fold both long raw edges to the centre and press. (You may find it easier to use a tape marker to do this.)

12 **Binding the tea cosy** Fold under 6mm (¼in) at one end of the binding and starting at the straight edge, pin binding to cover raw curved edge of cosy. Trim off excess binding, leaving 6mm (¼in) to turn under to neaten. Slipstitch the edges of the binding to the cosy.

13 **Attaching hanging loop** Cut an 8cm (3in) length of printed bias binding. Turn in ends then fold in half and stitch to centre of cosy top. Fold to wrong side 6mm (¼in) each end of bias strip, then fold in half lengthways and press. Fold to form a loop, then sew ends to top of tea-cosy.

Cheerful kitchen accessories

A co-ordinated set of pretty kitchen accessories will brighten up your kitchen by giving functional items a decorative look. Made in a fresh, easy-care fabric, the apron and matching oven gloves will protect your clothes and yourself from hot or messy foodstuffs without any compromise to good looks. The toaster cover, which can be made to fit any size or shape of toaster, completes the set.

Any strong, washable fabric can be used for the set. Pure cotton and linen look fresh and crisp, but do require more laundering than synthetic mixes. Polyester-cotton is a good choice because it combines the good looks of cotton with the easy care of polyester, however don't choose a lightweight polyester for the oven gloves, since these get the most wear, and need to be made from a strong fabric.

▲ Fresh delights
Made in a fabric depicting summer fruits, this lovely set of kitchen accessories looks delightfully fresh. A bold check, fresh gingham or polka dots would look equally appealing. Instructions for making the toaster cover and oven gloves will be in the next chapter.

APRON PATTERN PIECES

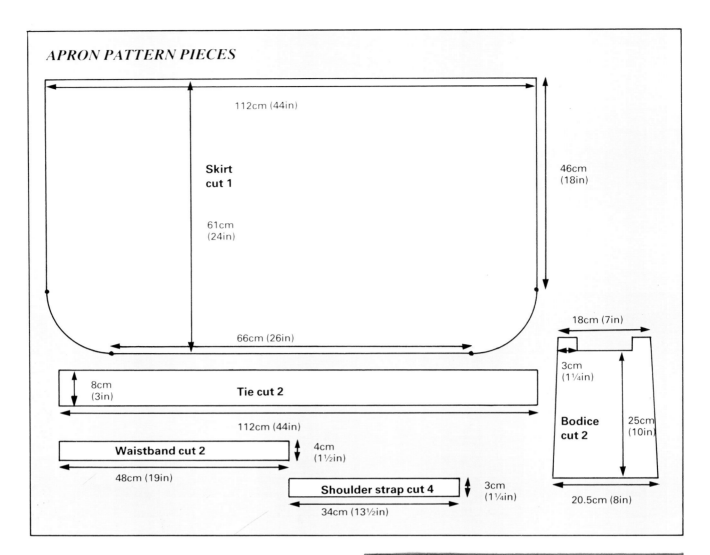

Skirt cut 1

112cm (44in)

61cm (24in)

46cm (18in)

66cm (26in)

Tie cut 2

8cm (3in)

112cm (44in)

Waistband cut 2

4cm (1½in)

48cm (19in)

Shoulder strap cut 4

3cm (1¼in)

34cm (13½in)

18cm (7in)

3cm (1¼in)

Bodice cut 2

25cm (10in)

20.5cm (8in)

Materials

Furnishing fabric at least 120cm (48in) wide: 1.5m (1 ⅝yd) for the apron; 70cm (¾yd) for the oven gloves, and 30cm (⅜yd) for the toaster cover.

12mm (½in) wide **bias binding**: 4.7m (5¼yd) for the apron; 1.7m (1 ⅞yd) for the oven gloves, and 2m (2¼yd) for a small toaster cover.

0.25m (¼yd) **cotton bump** or flannel to add insulation to the oven gloves.

Sewing thread to match both the binding and fabric.

MAKING THE APRON

1 Cutting out Draw up the patterns from the graph on to brown paper. Cut out, adding seam allowances of 1cm (⅜in) all round. For the bodice frill, cut two strips of fabric 5cm (2in) wide and 91cm (36in) long, and for the skirt frill, cut and join strips 8cm (3¼in) wide to make up a piece 300cm (120in) long; these frill pieces include seam allowances.

2 Making the skirt frill Join the skirt frill pieces together to make one long strip. Trim to a rounded shape at each end by drawing round a cup. Turn a double 5mm (¼in) hem to the wrong side along the curved edge and machine stitch.

3 Attaching the frill Divide the sides and lower edge of the skirt into four and mark. Repeat for the raw edge of the frill. Run two rows of gathering stitches along the raw edge of the frill and gather up to fit the skirt with marks matching, starting 1cm (⅜in) from the top. Pin with right sides facing and stitch, taking a 1cm (⅜in) seam allowance. Neaten the raw edges with zigzag.

4 Finishing the frill Press out the frill and press seam allowances towards the bodice. Pin bias binding over the seam, with the two long edges of the binding turned under. Topstitch in place close to each edge of the binding.

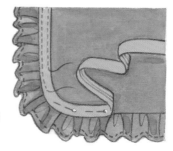

5 Attaching straps
With right sides facing, pin one short end of each shoulder strap to the top edge of each bodice. Stitch in place taking a 1cm (⅜in) seam allowance, then press the seam allowances open.

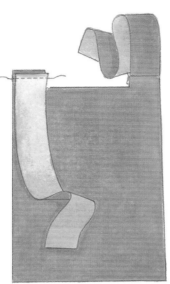

6 Bodice frills
Curve off the corners of each bodice frill and pin and then stitch a double 5mm (¼in) hem along the curved edge, as in step 2. Run two rows of gathering stitches along the remaining raw edge and gather up to fit the outer edges of one of the bodice pieces leaving a 1cm (⅜in) gap at each end – this is the front. Pin with right sides facing and stitch taking a 1cm (⅜in) seam.

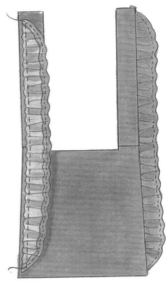

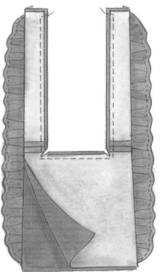

7 Bodice lining
With right sides facing, pin the bodice front (with the frill) to the bodice lining (without the frill). Stitch round the inner edge, taking a 1cm (⅜in) seam allowance. Snip to the stitching in the seam allowance at the corners and turn right side out.

8 Making the ties
Fold each tie in half lengthways, right sides facing. Pin and then stitch across one end and along the long edge. Trim the seam allowances at the corner and then turn right side out and press.

◄ Back view
The apron straps cross over at the back and pass through the binding loops on the waistband for a secure fit.

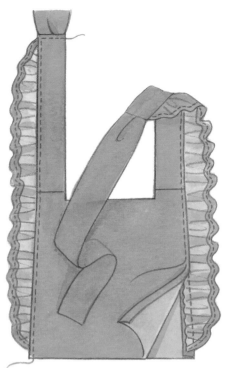

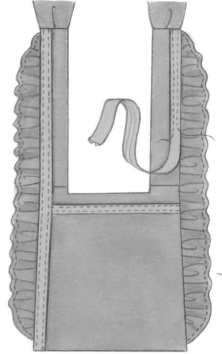

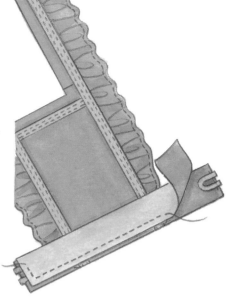

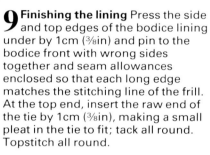

9 **Finishing the lining** Press the side and top edges of the bodice lining under by 1cm (3/8in) and pin to the bodice front with wrong sides together and seam allowances enclosed so that each long edge matches the stitching line of the frill. At the top end, insert the raw end of the tie by 1cm (3/8in), making a small pleat in the tie to fit; tack all round. Topstitch all round.

10 **Binding the bodice** Cut a length of binding long enough to go from one frill seam to the other on the bodice. Pin and then stitch to the top of the bodice 1cm (3/8in) from the top edge. Do not finish the ends. Cut two lengths of binding the length of the bodice and strap plus 1cm (3/8in). Turn 1cm (3/8in) under at one end and pin over the frill seam, with the neatened end at the top. Stitch in place along both long edges and across the top.

11 **Making the waistband** Cut an 18cm (7in) length of binding and fold in half lengthways, with the long edges turned inside. Pin and then stitch along the long edges. Cut into two equal lengths to make the loops. Position the waistband pieces right sides facing and raw edges level, with the loops sandwiched in between at each end and the bodice sandwiched in the middle. Starting 1cm (3/8in) from one long edge, pin and then stitch across the ends and along the other long edge, taking a 1cm (3/8in) seam allowance. Turn right side out and press in place.

Binding ease
When topstitching binding or ribbon along both edges, always stitch along each side in the same direction. The binding may stretch slightly as you sew, and if you stitch the sides in different directions it can cause wrinkles.

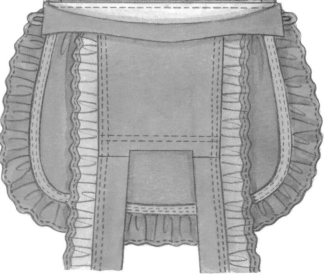

12 **Attaching the skirt** Run two rows of gathering stitches either side of the stitching line, 1cm (3/8in) from the top of the skirt. Pull up to fit the waistband with centres matching. Pin the skirt to the front edge of the top waistband, with right sides facing. Stitch, taking a 1cm (3/8in) seam allowance. On the inside, tuck the seam allowances on the free edge of the waistband under and pin. Slipstitch closed to finish.

Kitchen companions

These handy oven gloves and pretty toaster cover can be made to match the apron for a complete kitchen set. Both are easy to make, with the seams neatly enclosed in bias binding.

The oven gloves have an insulating layer of bump or flannel on both sides to protect your palms from hot dishes and the backs of your hands from the sides of the oven. Do not be tempted to use polyester wadding instead of the bump or flannel as this does not provide as much insulation.

The toaster cover can be made to fit any size or shape of toaster, although you may need to add a little extra ease if the toaster has rounded sides. Fabric requirements are given on page 24.

▲ Cherry ripe
For a country feel, make these pretty kitchen accessories in a fabric with a rural theme. The fruits on this toaster cover and oven gloves are ideal and look good enough to eat.

MAKING THE TOASTER COVER

1 Cutting out Measure the width, length and height of the toaster. Cut two side pieces the width of the toaster plus 2.5cm (1in) by the height plus 1.2cm (½in). Round off the top corners to match the shape of the toaster, if required. Cut the centre panel the depth of the toaster plus 2.5cm (1in) by the width plus twice the height of the side piece.

2 Stitching main seams With wrong sides facing, pin the centre panel to one side piece. Snip into the seam allowance of the centre panel at corners for ease and trim the end to fit. Tack and then stitch, taking a 1cm (⅜in) seam allowance. Stitch the other side of the centre panel to the second side piece.

3 Binding the edges Pin bias binding over the seam allowances on each side, covering the previous stitches – you may need to trim the seam allowances slightly. Do not turn the binding ends under. Tack close to the inner edges of the binding, then stitch through all thicknesses, following the tacking.

4 Binding the base Pin and then tack a strip of binding all round the lower edge of the cover in the same way. Overlap the binding where the two ends meet and turn the top end under to neaten. Stitch in place, remove all tacking stitches and then lightly press to finish.

MAKING THE OVEN GLOVES

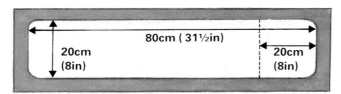

1 Cutting out To make a pattern, cut a piece of paper 20 x 80cm (8 x 31½in). Fold in half widthways and round off the ends by drawing round a plate or saucer. Unfold the pattern and use to cut two pieces of fabric. Cut the pattern 20cm (8in) from one end and use this to cut four pieces of fabric and four of bump or flannel.

2 Binding the ends With right sides outside, sandwich a piece of bump or flannel between a pair of small end pieces; tack all round. Repeat for the other pair of end pieces. Pin, tack and then stitch binding to the straight raw edge of each pair.

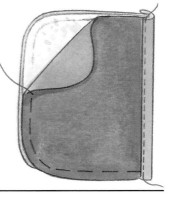

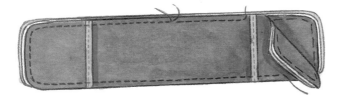

3 Making the gloves With right sides out, sandwich a piece of bump at each end between the two main pieces, with edges matching; pin. Place the two end pieces on top, with curved edges matching and tack. Remove pins and stitch close to the raw edges.

4 Binding the edges Pin binding round the edge of the oven gloves with the ends butting at the centre of one long edge. Tack and then stitch in place.

5 Making a hanging loop Cut a length of binding 10cm (4in) long. Fold in half lengthways, with long raw edges turned in, and stitch together close to the edge. Fold in half and pin to the binding next to the join in the edge binding. Stitch in place with two rows of stitching for strength and to prevent fraying. Remove tacking.

Appliqué towels

Appliqué perse is the simple technique of cutting a motif from a ready-printed fabric and applying it to a background. It is the quickest and easiest way to achieve an appliqué design, as the hard work of drawing each individual shape to create a design has been removed. All you need to do is cut out the printed motifs, following their outlines, and pin the shapes in a pleasing arrangement on your chosen fabric. Once in place, hand or machine stitch round the outer edges. Completed motifs can be embroidered or decorated with beads and trims.

This technique can be used all round the house – add motifs on to cushions and along the edges of curtains or sheets and pillow cases, taking the motifs from a fabric already used in the room, or team your bathroom or guest towels to match the curtains. Whatever the project or the fabric, the appliqué method remains the same.

▼ A pastel collection
The motifs of a cotton fabric were used on these towels. The motifs can be set in a band, centred or worked round a corner using separate flowers arranged together.

Materials

towels in chosen sizes and colours
floral fabric – choose a piece with distinctive motifs and the same care properties as the towels
dressmaker's marking pencil

fusible web backing (bondaweb)
sewing threads, to match the motifs and to match the towel. Work with the thread that matches the motif on the spool and the thread that matches the towel on the

bobbin. In this way the stitching will not stand out on the wrong side of the towel. If you want to define the edges of a motif use a thread which is a shade or so darker than the fabric.

HOW TO APPLIQUÉ THE TOWELS

1 Outline the motifs Select which flower motifs to use from the patterned fabric and draw round them on the right side of the fabric using a dressmaker's marking pencil. A single flower with a leaf or groups of flowers can be used. Roughly cut out each one, allowing spare fabric all round.

2 Back the motifs Place each motif on the bondaweb and cut out a piece to the same size. Iron the matching piece of bondaweb to the wrong side of the motif. Repeat for the number of motifs. Carefully trim each motif 3mm (¹⁄₈in) beyond the outline.

3 Arrange the motifs Position the motifs on the towel, moving them about until the arrangement looks good. The motifs can be overlapped or spaced out across the towel. Peel off the bondaweb backing and pin each motif in place on the towel. If the motifs are small, a single pin in the centre will be sufficient to hold them. Iron to fix each motif in place. Remove pins.

4 Stitching the edges Using a hand running stitch or machine straight stitch and, following the marked outline, stitch round the edge of each motif to hold in place. Set the sewing machine to a satin stitch of suitable width and carefully work round each motif in turn. Make sure that you cover the raw edges and the straight stitching.

5 Finishing off When the satin stitching is complete, take all the working threads to the wrong side and knot to fasten off.

Choosing the stitch length
Before satin stitching the outer edges, work a test piece, using a spare sample of the motif fabric on a similar background fabric – for example, a old flannel instead of a towel. Change the width of the stitch until you reach one that looks in proportion to the size of the motif.

▶ *A single motif*
Try the technique first on a hand towel using a single flower.

Lined baskets

Baskets are useful and decorative storage containers, and will add an instant country feel to any room. To give them a soft, attractive finish, edge with a quick frill in a crisp, cotton fabric tied to the handles of the baskets with two lengths of narrow satin ribbon. Use them in the kitchen to store vegetables, tea towels, cooking utensils or just fill with dried flowers.

For a really special finish, a quilted, fitted lining is ideal, particularly if the basket is prominently displayed or if it will store delicate items. A bread basket, used on the breakfast table, for example, looks great with a fitted, quilted lining. It's practical too, if made with flaps which will cover the freshly baked rolls or croissants to protect them and keep them warm.

▲ *Bread basket*
To keep freshly-baked rolls or croissants warm, nothing could be nicer than a basket with warm, quilted fabric in bright and cheerful colours to enliven the breakfast table and get the day off to a really good start.

A lined basket

Materials

Although not difficult to sew, a fitted lining can be fiddly, so start with a basket which has a simple shape, and take special care making the pattern. Use **brown paper** for the pattern, rather than newspaper which can dirty the fabric, and to save time and effort use **ready-quilted fabric** for the main lining. You will also need a **second fabric** for the inner lining plus **ribbon** for the bow trim. Bind the flaps, with **bias binding strips** cut from the lining fabric, or buy wide ready-made binding to match.

MAKING A LINED BASKET

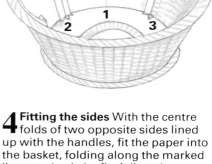

1 Pattern for the base Place a piece of brown paper in the bottom of the basket and press it down on to the base. Crease along the edge of the base with your finger, then cut along the crease to make the pattern. Since the basket is unlikely to be completely symmetrical, replace the pattern and mark the position of the handles to help positioning later.

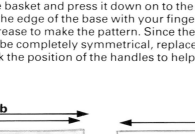

2 Pattern for the sides Measure the depth of the sides (**a**), then measure the top circumference of the basket and divide into four (**b**). On brown paper, draw four rectangles the depth of the sides by a quarter of the circumference and cut out, leaving an extra 1cm (⅜in) all round for adjustment. Fold each rectangle in half lengthways and press the foldline, then unfold.

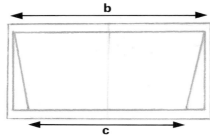

3 Shaping the sides Measure the circumference of the base on the inside of the basket and divide into four (**c**). Mark this measurement on the lower edge of each rectangle, with the measurement centred across the fold. Draw a diagonal line joining the ends of the top and bottom lines, then trim 1cm (⅜in) outside the diagonal lines.

4 Fitting the sides With the centre folds of two opposite sides lined up with the handles, fit the paper into the basket, folding along the marked lines to check the fit. Adjust the pieces to fit together exactly, trimming off the excess paper. Each piece may be slightly different, so give each one a number, and mark the base to correspond. Mark the base with notches where the side seams will meet it.

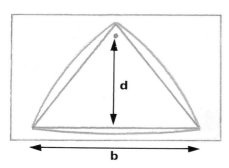

5 Pattern for the flaps On a piece of brown paper, draw a triangle with the lower edge the same width as the upper edge of one side piece (**b**), and the upper point the distance from the edge to the centre of the basket (**d**) plus 2.5cm (1in) away from it. Curve the sides quite fully, and give the lower edge a more gentle curve.

6 Cutting out From both lining and main fabric, cut out one base piece, four side pieces and four flap pieces – add 1.5cm (⅝in) seam allowances to all edges except the side edges of the flaps which will be bound. Make sure the pattern on the side and flap pieces is upright and match pattern repeats where possible. From lining fabric cut strips of 5mm (¼in) bias binding (see page 93) for the flaps.

Transfer all markings from the pattern to the wrong side of the fabric pieces with tailor's chalk.

7 Stitching the sides Tack the side pieces of main fabric together along the short edges, taking a 1.5cm (⅝in) seam allowance, and stopping 1.5cm (⅝in) from the lower edge. Check the fit in the basket, and pin any adjustments necessary. Stitch the seams, then press them open.

◄ Fresh surprise
The pretty flaps on this bread basket are insulated with quilted fabric to keep the bread warm. Place the filled basket on the table with the flaps closed, and then open them out to delight the whole family with the irresistible aroma of the freshly baked bread.

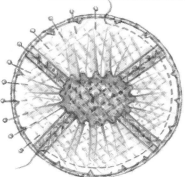

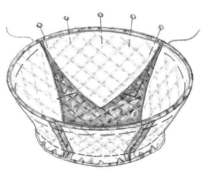

8 **Attaching the base** Snip into the lower seam allowance on the side pieces at 2.5cm (1in) intervals for ease. Pin to the base piece, right sides together, and raw edges matching; tack 1.5cm (⅝in) from the raw edge. Check the fit in the basket and adjust if necessary, then stitch the seam all round.

9 **Attaching the flaps** With the raw edges of the flaps matching the side seams on the side pieces and with right sides facing, tack a flap to the top of each side piece, easing the flap to fit and trimming the flaps slightly at the side edges if necessary for a good fit; stitch.

10 **Making the lining** Repeat steps 7-9 to make up the lining. With wrong sides together, place the lining inside the main piece, and pin together with seams matching. Smooth flat – the lining may be slightly larger than the main piece at the raw edges. Pin edges then stitch together 5mm (¼in) from the raw edge of the flaps on the main piece. Trim the lining as necessary.

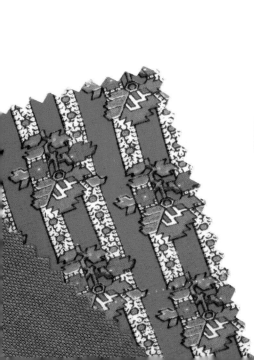

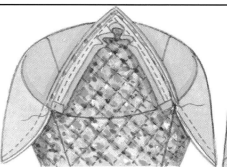

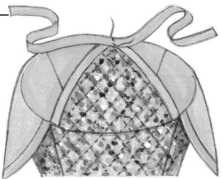

11 **Binding the flaps** Cut a piece of binding at least 2cm (¾in) longer than the curved edge of each flap – allow a little extra to be sure you have enough. Turn one end of the binding under 1cm (⅜in) and pin in position on the right side of the main fabric; turn the other end under by 1cm (⅜in) to neaten. Stitch along the first fold in the binding.

12 **Finishing off** Turn the binding to the lining side and slipstitch in place. Fold a piece of ribbon in half and stitch the fold to the main fabric at the point of one flap, tie the ribbon in a bow and trim the ends at an angle. When you close the flaps, this flap should be on top. Add additional bow trims, attached to the basket at the corners.

A quick frill

Materials

A quick, gathered frill will transform a **plain basket** at little cost. About 1m (1yd) of **fabric** or even less will be sufficient to make a frill for most handy baskets, and you may be able to make it from a remnant. You will also need enough 8-10mm (¼-⅜in) **ribbon** to go round the circumference of the basket plus 120cm (48in) to tie to the handles.

MAKING A QUICK FRILL

1 Cutting out Decide on the finished depth of the frill – the one shown right is 12cm (4¾in) deep. Add 7cm (2¾in) for hem and casing allowances and cut out strips of fabric this deep by the full width of the fabric to make up a piece 2½-3 times the circumference of the basket at the top. There must be a seam at each end at the handles so that the ribbon can be drawn out of the casings and tied on to the handles, so either cut an even number of strips, or cut one strip in half.

▲ Quick frill
A gathered frill, tied on with pretty ribbon, adds instant charm to a simple, rustic basket. It is easy and quick to make, and can be co-ordinated with your kitchen.

2 Joining the strips Pin and then stitch the strips together to make up a ring, but on two opposite seams leave the upper end of the seam open by 4cm (1½in). This will provide an opening in the casing for the ribbon which ties on to the handles of the basket.

3 Hemming the frill Turn 2cm (¾in) and then another 2cm (¾in) to the wrong side along the bottom edge of the frill to make a double hem and tack or pin, then stitch in place by hand or machine; press.

5 Finishing off Cut the ribbon in half and thread one piece along the casing on half the frill, using a safety pin to thread it through. Thread the other piece through the other half of the casing so that the ribbon ends emerge at the gaps in the casing on two opposite sides of the frill. Gather up and tie on to the handles of the basket, then tie in a bow and trim the ribbon ends at an angle to finish.

4 Making the casings At the top of the frill turn 1cm (½in) and then 2cm (¾in) to the wrong side. Pin and stitch close to the fold, ensuring there is enough depth in the casing above the stitches for the ribbon.

Fabric picture frames

Fabric-covered picture frames are a pretty and economical alternative to wooden frames, and will really draw attention to the pictures. Only the frame has to be covered in the main fabric, so the minimum of fabric is required, and you could probably use light to medium-weight fabric left over from other soft furnishings in the room. Dressmaking fabrics work particularly well, including silks and cottons, so there should be no problem finding an appropriate fabric for your frame.

If the picture is going to be hung, a short length of co-ordinating satin ribbon can be inserted between the frame and the back to hang the picture from. However, if the picture is to be placed on a table, it is necessary to make a back stand to prop up the picture.

▲ Perfect pair
These pressed flower pictures have splendid padded frames in damask fabric which picks up the colours from the wallpaper for perfect co-ordination. The tasselled cord completes the elegant effect.

Materials

Furnishing fabric(s) to cover the frame and/or mount. For the lining you can either use a separate, cheaper fabric or simply use more of the main fabric.
Squared paper for a pattern.
Stiff card for the frame and back of the picture frame.
Multi-purpose **glue** such as Copydex.
Fusible webbing such as Bondaweb.
Light to mediumweight **wadding (batting)**
Narrow ribbon to hang the picture with.
Plastic sheeting (optional) such as Artcell to protect the picture.

SIMPLE PICTURE FRAME

1 Making a pattern Using the picture as a guide, make a full-size pattern of the finished frame. Cut out the centre, remembering that wide frames are stronger and less fiddly to cover than narrow ones, so start with one at least 3cm (1¼in) deep.

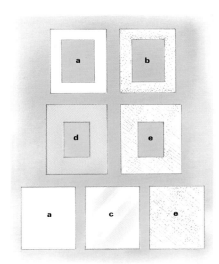

2 Cutting out Cut a piece of card round the outside of the pattern for the back. Cut out a second piece, but this time cut round the inner line as well to make the frame. From lining fabric cut a piece the same size as the back, and from wadding cut a piece the size of the frame. From main fabric cut one piece 2cm (¾in) larger than the frame. From fusible webbing cut one piece the same as the fabric frame, and one the size of the lining. You should have two pieces of card (**a**), one of wadding (**b**), one of lining (**c**), one of main fabric and two of fusible webbing (**e**).

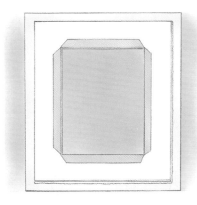

3 Making the frame Take the card frame and glue the polyester wadding to it. Fuse the webbing to the wrong side of the fabric frame. Peel off the backing and place the fabric frame right side down on the ironing board. Centre the wadding side of the card frame on top. Snip into the fabric at the inner corners and then carefully iron the excess fabric on to the back of the card on the inside edges only. Iron the fabric to the wadding on the front of the frame to hold, but do not secure the outer allowances.

4 Inserting the picture Carefully position the picture in the frame. If it is smaller than the outer edge of the frame, stick it to the inside of the frame to hold it in place.

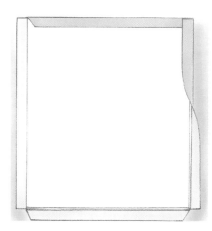

5 Joining the frame Place the remaining card on to the back of the picture and frame. Ease the outer fabric allowance of the frame to the back, encasing all layers, and fuse in place with the iron. Trim the fabric allowances at the corners so the fabric lies flat.

6 Lining the back Glue a piece of ribbon about a quarter of the way from each side on the top edge for hanging. Fuse the webbing on to the wrong side of the lining and then fuse the other side to the back, covering the fused allowances of the main fabric and the ends of the ribbon. The fusible webbing will prevent the lining from fraying.

tip

Protective cover
To protect a favourite photograph in the frame, insert a sheet of clear plastic, such as Artcell in front of the picture. Lighter than glass and certainly not as difficult to use, clear plastic is an excellent alternative to picture glass.

RE-USABLE FRAME

The simple picture frame looks really pretty, particularly when several are arranged together, but once you have inserted the picture, it cannot be changed. This is not usually a problem, but if the frame is designed as a present, it can be made so that the picture can be inserted or changed later.

1 Cutting out Make a pattern as in step 1 for a simple picture frame and cut out the same pieces as in step 2. In addition, cut a piece from main fabric and fusible webbing the size of the card back plus 2cm (¾in) all round and a piece from lining and fusible webbing the same size as the card frame.

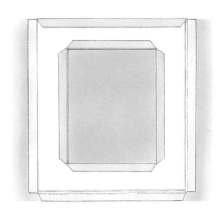

2 Making the frame Glue the wadding frame to the card and leave to dry thoroughly. Fuse the webbing to the wrong side of the main fabric frame and then peel off the protective backing. Place the card frame, wadding side down on top of the fabric and snip into the fabric allowances at the corners. Iron the allowances to the card on the inside of the frame and along the top outside edge only.

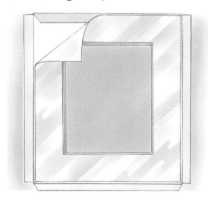

3 Finishing the frame Iron the fusible webbing to the wrong side of the lining frame. Peel off the backing and then iron on to the card frame, covering all fabric allowances except the three outside allowances which should be left free.

4 Making the back Iron the fusible backing on to the wrong side of the main back fabric. Remove the protective backing and then iron on to the remaining card. Turn the allowances to the wrong side of the card and iron these down too.

5 Assembling the frame Place the right side of the back to the wrong side of the frame and fold the free fabric allowances from the frame to the back; fuse to the back. Glue ribbon to the back for hanging as in step 6 for simple picture frames.

6 Adding the lining Fuse the webbing to the wrong side of the lining for the back and then iron this to the back of the card, covering the seam allowances. Slip the picture into place through the gap in the top of the frame.

Fabric mounts

Fabric-covered mounts make a lovely alternative to coloured card and can be used in conjunction with wooden or fabric-covered frames. You could even dispense with the frame and use the mount as a combined mount and frame.

Ready-made card mounts with one or more shapes cut out for the photographs can be bought from picture framing shops and from some haberdashery departments. These simplify making fabric mounts, but you can cut your own from mounting card, available from art shops.

MAKING A FABRIC MOUNT

1 Cutting out Purchase or make a mount from mounting card. Cut the fabric 2cm (¾in) larger all round, including the same allowance on the inside edges of the shapes. Cut fusible webbing the same size as the fabric and fuse to the wrong side of the fabric. If the frame is re-usable, cut lining fabric the same size as the mount.

2 Making the mount Peel the webbing's protective backing off, then place the card centrally on top. Snip into the fabric allowances at curves and trim at corners. Carefully fuse these allowances to the wrong side, ensuring there are no creases on the right side, then turn the card over and fuse to the right side. Fuse the lining over the back, if needed.

MAKING A SHAPED FRAME

Making the frame Cut out the card and fabric as for a fabric mount, but also cut out a piece of wadding the same size as the card. Glue the wadding to the card, and make a back piece as for a simple or re-usable picture frame. Follow the instructions for the type of frame you are making – simple or re-usable – to complete.

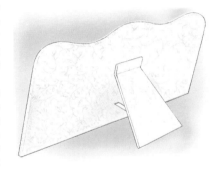

▲ *Back stand*
A back stand is ideal for table-top photographs.

▲ *Two colour damask*
A fabric mount within a padded fabric frame – the cord makes a mock mitre at the corners.

Back stand

If the picture is not going to be hung, it will require a back stand so that it can be placed on a flat surface, such as a bedside table. This is easy to make and requires only a small piece of card, a scrap of the fabric and some fusible webbing and thread.

MAKING A BACK STAND

1 Cutting out Cut a piece of card 4cm (1½in) wide and 1cm (½in) deep. Cut a second piece half the height of the frame and 6cm (2¼in) wide. Trim the larger piece equally on each side so that it tapers to 4cm (1½in) at the top end. Cut a rectangle of fabric and fusible webbing 8cm (3in) wide and the length of the two pieces of card together plus 2cm (¾in).

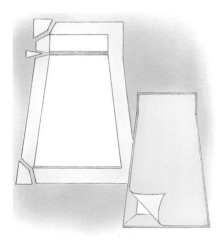

2 Covering the stand Fuse the webbing to the back of the fabric and remove the backing. Place both pieces of card centrally on the wrong side of the fabric with a small gap, no deeper than the thickness of the card, between them. Trim the seam allowances to 1.5cm (⅝in) all round. Fold the seam allowances over, snipping into the allowances for ease, and then fuse to hold. Fuse on the right side too.

3 Lining the stand Cut a piece of lining and fusible webbing the size of the stand. Fuse the webbing to the lining and then fuse the lining to back of the stand.

4 Attaching the stand Glue the top of the stand to the back of the frame so that when the lower end is angled away from the frame, it is level with the bottom. To hold the stand in place, attach a chain of plaited thread, glued to the back of the stand and to the frame.

DECORATIVE IDEAS

Mock mitres Glue strips of Russian braid from the centre corners of the frame to the outside corners before attaching the lining for the back.

Piping trim Cut and cover strips of piping long enough to go round the inside and outside edges of the frame. Glue to the wrong side of the frame on the inside edge before attaching the back, and to the outside edge before attaching the lining. Snip into the fabric covering the piping at corners for ease.

▲ **Variety show**
Create a variety of effects with padded picture frames.

Lace edge Use lace with one finished edge, and cut enough lace to go round the outside of the frame. Glue it to the back before attaching the back lining. For lace with two finished edges, glue the lace to the back of the frame once it is completed.

Fitted lampshades

Fitted lampshades are an elegant addition to graceful lamp bases and light fittings, and look particularly good in dining rooms, living rooms and formal bedrooms. Despite their tailored appearance, they are deceptively easy to make, and you don't need to be a neat seamstress either, since the hand stitching is covered with a trimming such as binding or braid.

A lining on such a shade is optional, but it provides a professional finish by concealing the frame and the raw edges of the seams in the main fabric. It also helps to block out the outline of the bulb and struts when the light is on, and reflects light, giving the finished effect greater brilliance.

Bowed lampshades

Fitted lampshades come in many shapes and sizes – panelled, bowed, tiffany style and with straight or scalloped edges – but of all these, the bowed shape is perhaps the easiest to fit and also one of the most widely used. These shades have circular rings at the top and bottom, with the top ring either the same size or smaller than the bottom one. The sides are panelled off by struts which curve inwards, giving the shade a very elegant appearance.

Fabric selection

Even if the shade is lined, this sort of cover does not require a great deal of fabric, but you do need to make your choice carefully. Soft, easily draped fabric such as fine cotton, silk, satin and crêpe are best for both the main fabric and lining. Stiff fabrics with no stretch should be avoided, as should fabrics which fray easily.

Since the fabric is used on the bias, patterns with an obvious direction should be avoided. For this reason, most fitted lampshades are made from plain fabrics, but some all-over patterns, miniprints and checks can be used if you prefer. Hold the fabric up by the corner to see if the pattern looks good from this angle – if so, you can use it. Remember that even plain fabrics sometimes have a woven pattern, so check these fabrics on the diagonal too.

The fabric colour you choose should go with the colour of the lamp base and décor of the room, but for maximum light reflection, select a paler lining fabric to go with it. If the main fabric is cream or white, with a matching lining, it will radiate a bright light, while a warm colour such as yellow, pale pink or peach will emit a more comfortable glow, making these a good choice for bedrooms or sitting rooms.

▼ Stretch fit
Most plain fabrics and some patterned ones can be used to cover bowed lampshades, but they should have a fair amount of stretch on the bias.

Materials

Bowed lampshade frame.
Furnishing fabric.
Stretchy lining fabric.
Matching thread.
Trimmings.
Pins and needle.
Tailor's chalk.
Fabric glue to attach the trimmings.

BOWED LAMPSHADE

1 Preparation Buy a lampshade frame of the size you want, or remove the old fabric cover from an existing shade. Tape the struts and rings firmly with strong, white cotton tape to make a base on which to stitch the fabric cover (see page 94).

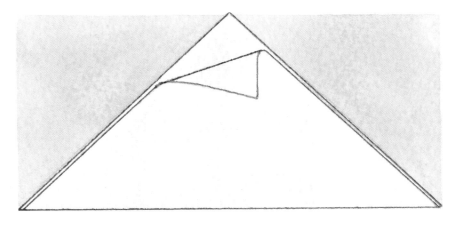

2 Cutting out Cut a square of fabric on the straight grain, which, when folded into a triangle from corner to corner, will cover half the lampshade with a 4cm (1½in) overlap all round.

A square, one and a half times the length of one strut, should be sufficient, but if the top ring is large, you may require more. Cut lining fabric to the same size.

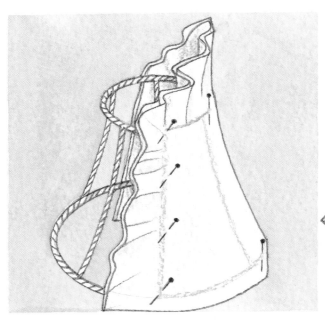

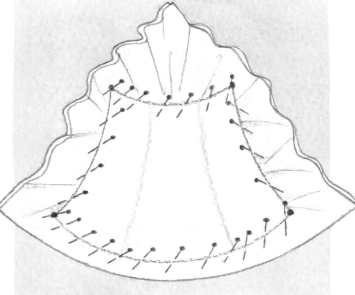

3 Pinning the fabric With the main fabric folded into a triangle, right sides together, and with the fold parallel to the bottom ring, pin the doubled fabric to the frame at the top and bottom of two opposite struts. Pull the fabric taut and add further pins at the centre of the fabric on each of the two struts and each ring. Add more pins in between and adjust the fabric until all wrinkles are smoothed out.

4 Marking the fabric With tailor's chalk, draw along the fabric directly over the two end struts, then mark the position of the top and bottom rings where they meet the struts. Draw lightly along the pinned line of the top and bottom rings. Pin the fabric together at the edges to hold, then carefully remove the pins that fix it to the frame.

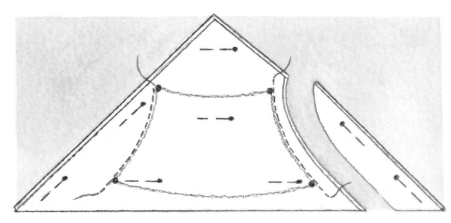

5 Stitching side seams Still with the fabric pinned together, extend the chalk line by 2cm (¾in) on each end, then stitch along the chalk lines. Trim away the excess fabric along the two sides, leaving a 1cm (⅜in) seam allowance. Trim along the top and bottom edges, leaving a 1.5cm (⅝in) gap between the marked line and the edge.

6 Making the lining Fold the lining into a triangle, right sides together, and pull on the two ends to ease out the stretch. Matching the straight grain of lining and main fabric, pin the main fabric to the lining and trim the lining to the same size. Stitch the two side seams, taking a 1.3cm (½in) seam allowance. This makes the lining piece slightly smaller than the main fabric to allow for it being inside the frame. Press the seams open on lining and fabric.

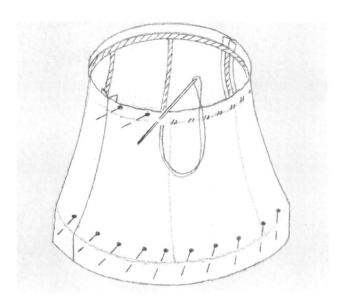

7 Fitting the cover Turn the main piece right side out and slip over the taped frame. Position the two seams exactly over a strut with the marks matching the rings at each end. Pin the fabric to the struts round both rings, pulling smooth to ease out any wrinkles. Using a double thread, oversew the fabric to the tape on the top and bottom rings. The stitches will be covered by the lining or trimmings later. Trim the surplus fabric close to stitching.

8 Positioning lining Slip the lining into the frame, with the right side facing inside. Pin roughly in position with the seams matching the seams on the main fabric and with excess fabric overlapping the frame.

▲ *Inside story*
A lining gives a fitted lampshade a professional finish, and the strip of lining which neatens the area around the gimbal is the final touch.

10 Attaching the lining Bring the lining over the rings to the outside and oversew to the rings with a double thread in the same way as the main fabric. If trimming with braid or ribbon, ensure the stitches are on the front of the shade, rather than the top so that the trimming will cover them. Trim away surplus fabric close to the stitching and glue on a trimming (see next page).

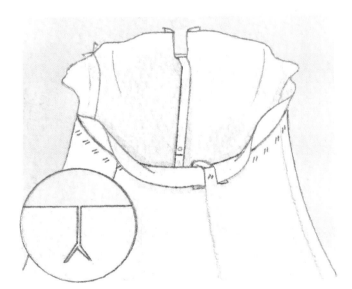

9 At the fitting The upper ring has a light fitting, called a gimbal, round which the lining must be fitted. Mark the position of the underside of the gimbal. Cut the fabric centrally to a point 1cm (⅜in) above it, then cut diagonal slits to each corner. Turn the fabric under at the gimbal to neaten, then finish pinning the lining to the rings, pulling out any remaining wrinkles as you do so.

tip

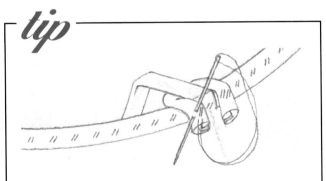

Professional gimbal edge
To finish the lining round the gimbal like an expert, cut two strips of excess lining fabric 2.5cm (1in) wide and 5cm (2in) long. Fold the two long edges of each strip to the centre, then fold in half lengthways. Wrap the strip under the gimbal and stitch to the top of the ring on each side; trim.

DECORATIVE TRIMMINGS

Binding To make your own bias binding, follow the instructions on page 93. Alternatively use wide, ready-made bias binding. Turn the end of the binding to the wrong side, then with right sides facing, stitch the binding to the shade along the first fold, starting at a seam in the fabric. Turn back the other end of the binding. Flip the binding over to the lining side and glue or slipstitch in place.

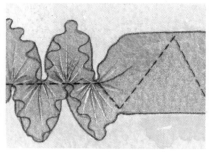

Ruched velvet Cut a length of velvet ribbon twice the length of each ring. Sew across the ribbon in a regular zigzag line taking small running stitches, and drawing up the ribbon at intervals until it fits the shade. Catchstitch the ribbon to the shade so that it slightly overlaps the edge, giving a scalloped effect.

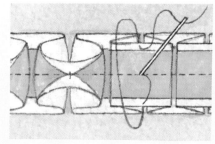

Pleated ribbon Cut two pieces of ribbon, three times the length of each ring, and stitch the narrower piece to the wider one along the middle. Fold the fabric into box pleats of equal size by pleating the fabric first one way and then the other; stitch. Pinch the box pleats together at the centre and catch the edges of the outer ribbon with a matching thread. Glue to the shade.

Braid or fringing Turn one end of the trimming under, then glue in position on the shade, starting at a seam on the fabric. Turn the other end under so that it butts up to the fold of the first end; glue. Bulldog clips can be used to hold the trimming in place while it dries.

A selection of tapes, ribbons and braids suitable for trimming lampshades.

Pleated fabric lampshades

Depending on the type of frame and choice of fabric, a pleated lampshade can take on a number of different looks, and be adapted to suit almost any setting. A plain fabric, pleated into even, crisp folds and mounted on a steeply sloping or drum-shaped frame, will create a shade whose sober charm will be ideal for a smart living or dining room, or a formal bedroom. A patterned fabric mounted on a gently sloping frame, like a coolie, will have a fresher and more modern feel, as the pleats will fan out towards the base of the shade to soften the overall effect.

When making your own lampshade you can afford to be selective, so take some time to choose a suitable fabric which will complement the room's colour scheme, style and existing furnishings. An easy option is simply to use the same fabric as the curtains and other existing soft furnishings, but do be wary of creating an overly co-ordinated look – most rooms really benefit from the spark of individuality which small accessories can bring.

Suitable fabrics

As pleated lampshades are often left unlined, try to choose a medium-weight fabric with a fairly dense weave; if the fabric is too fine or has an open weave, both the light bulb and frame will show through. However, thin fabrics can be used successfully if backed with a soft iron-on interfacing before being mounted on to the shade, or if the finished shade is lined. Avoid very thick fabrics, which will be difficult to pleat up

▲ Pleated from top to toe
A fresh floral print loosely pleated over a gently sloping frame makes a charming informal shade. A fabric-covered base completes the effect.

and will allow only a little light to filter through. Pleat up a patterned fabric before you buy it to check the finished effect.

When choosing fabric for making a lampshade, always consider the way in which it transmits light. Beware of some colours, particularly blues and greens, which can make a room feel cold. The safest bets are golden or reddish shades, like peach, apricot and yellow, which create a soft, warm and cosy glow. In the interests of safety, try to choose a non-flammable fabric.

43

Materials

Lampshade frame with vertical or sloping sides; avoid frames with bowed sides, waisted shapes or shaped edges.

Strong cotton tape for covering the struts and rings of the frame

Fabric to cover the frame (see step 2 for quantity)

Pins

Thimble

Matching thread

Bias binding 2cm (¾in) wide, to fit round the base and top rings of the frame, plus a little extra for ease; either buy ready-made binding, or make up binding from the same fabric as the shade (see page 93).

Fabric glue to attach the binding

PLEATED LAMPSHADE

These instructions are for an unlined lampshade with gently sloping sides. The fabric is marked off into a series of equal sections, which are pleated up and pinned in place one at a time; by working section by section, you can achieve a perfectly even finish and will find the fabric far easier to work with.

1 Preparing the frame If using the frame from an existing lampshade, first remove the old fabric. If necessary, bind the struts and rings of the frame with strong cotton tape – this will create a fabric base to which the fabric cover can then be stitched (for details see page 94).

2 Measuring up and cutting out Measure the circumference of the top ring, multiply this measurement by three, and add a further 6cm (2½in); make sure that this measurement is at least 1½ times the circumference of the base ring. Then measure the depth of the frame, from the top ring to the base ring, and add 6cm (2½in). Cut a rectangle of your fabric to these dimensions. Where you need to cut more than one width to create the required length, do not sew the widths together – they will be overlapped during pleating (see step 7). Allow an extra 5cm (2in) for each overlap.

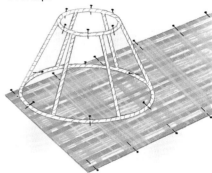

3 Sectioning the fabric Count the number of panels on the frame. Mark off a 3cm (1¼in) allowance at both short ends of the length of fabric, then divide it into the same number of sections as the frame, marking off each one with pins at the top and lower edges. Use a pin to mark the centre of each panel on the frame, and also the centre of each fabric section, on the top and lower edges.

4 Pinning the fabric to the frame Pin the first fabric section over one of the panels on the frame. Make sure that an equal fabric allowance extends beyond the top and base of the frame, and that the 3cm (1¼in) end allowance overlaps the side strut; line up the two section marks and the halfway marks on the fabric with two side struts and the centre point on the frame; pin the fabric in place on the frame.

◀ *Colourful checks*
With a little experimentation, tartans and checks can be used to great effect on pleated lampshades to create interesting patterns and strong bands of colour. Self-fabric binding cut on the bias to create diagonal checks provides a stylish finishing touch.

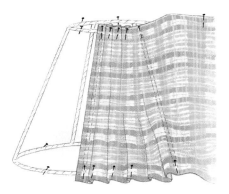

5 **Pleating up the fabric** Gauge how many pleats look best between each strut, and roughly pin in place along the top and bottom rings; adjust the fabric until you find an attractive arrangement, and make sure all the pleats are the same size.

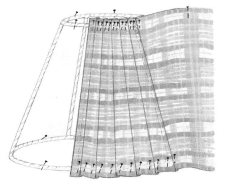

6 **Pinning the pleats in place** When satisfied with the number and size of the pleats, pin them neatly and securely in place along the top ring; the fold of the last pleat should just reach the second strut. To pin the pleats to the base ring, follow the foldline of each pleat down from the top ring, gently pressing it into a soft crease, but pleat up an increasingly small amount of fabric as you near the base ring; with the fabric stretched across the shade, pin each pleat in place. The pleats will then fan out evenly and attractively as the frame widens.

7 **Overlapping fabric widths** Repeat to pleat up the fabric between each strut in the same way. If you need to join on extra fabric widths, slip the edge of the new fabric piece into the last pleat, so that the join will not be visible on the right side of the shade. Then continue to pleat up as usual, making sure the join remains invisible as you fan out the pleats towards the base ring.

8 **A final check** When you reach the final pleat, trim any excess fabric, then pin the pleat in place over the fabric allowance left at the start, turning in the raw edges. Check that all the pleats around the shade are the same size, and make adjustments where necessary.

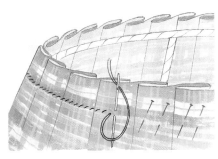

9 **Stitching the fabric to the frame** Using a double thread, oversew round the top of the frame from the outside, making sure each pleat is firmly stitched to the taped ring. Repeat round the bottom ring and remove all pins. Trim the excess fabric from just above the stitching on both the top and the base ring.

▲ A warm glow
Pleated shades in plain fabrics are an ideal choice for elegant settings.

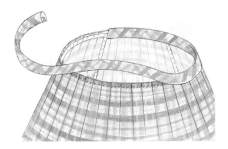

10 **Trimming the shade** Trim the shade with matching or contrast binding to conceal the raw edges. If you are binding in matching fabric, press the raw long edges of your bias strips to the wrong side. Then fold the binding in half lengthways, and glue in place over the raw edges of the fabric, to conceal the top and base rings. Position the binding end at the back of the shade over a strut and in line with the edge of a pleat; turn under 5mm (¼in) at the raw ends and butt together.

Pleated patterns
Using the same technique on a plain fabric, you can create striking pleated patterns, which will stand out when light is shone through the lampshade. Rather than pleating up the whole length of fabric, use a shorter strip and only pleat up groups of two or three pleats, leaving smooth gaps between each group; or create an attractive stripy effect by alternating between single pleats and spaces of the same width.

BOX-PLEATED LAMPSHADE

Box-pleated lampshades are a smart variation on ordinary pleated shades, and are made similarly.

1 Preparing the fabric Prepare a steep-sided or drum-shaped frame. Measure circumference of top ring, multiply by three, and add 6cm (2½in). Measure the depth of the shade and cut out fabric to this size. Divide fabric into sections, marking off allowances at both ends.

2 Marking up the pleats As box-pleats are more difficult to measure and fold evenly, you will find it easier to mark up their positions with tailor's chalk before the fabric is mounted on the shade. Divide the first section into a suitable number of pleats, remembering that each pleat takes three times as much fabric as its finished width. Check the finished effect by mounting the first section on the shade and pinning in place. Adjust the fabric until satisfied with the result.

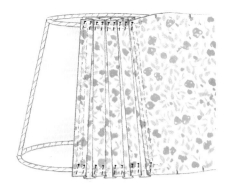

3 Pinning the fabric in place Once satisfied, remove the first section from the shade and mark up the other sections in the same way. Working on one section at a time and pleating the fabric according to the chalk marks, pin the fabric to the frame along the top and then the bottom ring; try to avoid opening up the pleats as you work towards the lower ring – to accommodate the shape of the frame, reduce the amount of fabric behind the pleat.

4 Finishing the shade Make a final check, then stitch the fabric to the shade as before. Cut away the excess fabric, and bind to finish.

◄ *Classically elegant*
Floral prints soften the tailored lines of a box-pleated shade.

▼ *Decorative detail*
Emphasize a smocked shade with ribbon bows in a contrasting shade.

SMOCKED LAMPSHADE

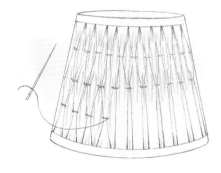

By smocking the pleats of a box-pleated shade, you can transform its tailored lines into ripples of soft folds, and create a wonderfully textured surface.

Starting near the top of the shade and working in a straight line around it, pinch each box pleat to the centre and secure with a few small stitches. Then measure a third to halfway down the shade (depending on its height) pull each pleat apart, and use small stitches to attach it to the neighbouring pleat. Measure an equal distance down the shade and stitch the pleats as for the top line of smocking. Continue with rows of smocking to just above lower ring.

Cushion collections

Cushions are the perfect finishing touch. They can enhance a colour theme, turn a dull room into a lively one, or transform an ordinary bedroom into a boudoir.

Cushions are an easy way to pull together the decorative scheme in a room. For instance, if you have patterned curtains, cushions of the same fabric on the sofa or chairs will add a co-ordinated touch; take the theme one step further by choosing two or three colours from the curtain pattern and buy or make scatter cushions in plain fabrics in these colours. If you have patterned upholstery, cushions in a toning or complementary plain colour will be effective but cushions in a distinctive accent colour will really draw the eye.

If your room has a neutral colour scheme then you can dramatize it with your choice of cushions. Try using lots of different fabrics and textures: silk, hessian, tapestry, velvet, patchwork, cotton, lace – the range is limitless. The remnant counters of fabric shops provide happy hunting grounds for cushion-sized pieces; all you need to take into consideration is the probable wear on your planned cushions – for instance, if you have children and pets you'll need to choose a washable fabric.

▲ Love-knot variations
The pillows on this attractive button-backed bed are decorated with appliqued bows cut from the fabric used for the headboard. Tiny cushions are either covered in old lace to match the lace-edged sheets or stencilled following the same design theme.

The co-ordinated look ▶
The colour scheme of the room is based on creamy apricot walls and blue wood furniture. The plain lines of the sofa are softened with a mass of co-ordinating scatter cushions – a framework of large square cushions supports three smaller circular ones. Floral gingham and patterned chintz pick up the apricot and blue and add a warm accent of coral.

▲ **Cushioned cane**
A low cane chair is attractively decorated and softened with an appliqued cushion. The garland is done by the appliqué perse method (see pages 29-30) where the motif is cut from a patterned fabric and applied to a plain background.

◀ **Under the eaves**
A plain attic room with a simple iron bedstead is magically transformed into a pretty Victorian bedroom with piles of deeply-frilled, lace-edged cushions.

Patchwork cushion

The craft of patchwork has been used for centuries to make use of odd scraps of fabric around the home. Many of the patch shapes and arrangements are complicated but the square patch used for this cushion is a very basic shape and can be sewn together by hand, using a small oversew stitch, or by machine making the patchwork effect very quick and simple to achieve. All fabrics used, in one item should be either of cotton or a cotton mix, with a similar weight and the same care instructions. It is advisable to collect all the fabrics that will be used first, and then wash and iron them before beginning the work.

▼ **Square patches**
The cushion has been made in a blue and pink colour scheme, but you could choose colours to suit your bedroom. Once you have mastered the craft of patchwork you may decide to make the quilt too.

Materials

Cotton polyester fabric 25 patches in a selection of light colours and 24 patches in a selection of dark colours, each measuring 8cm (3¼in) square

Cotton polyester fabric of the same weight and laundering instructions to match the dominant dark colour of patches 44cm (17¼in) square

Sewing thread in both light and dark shades

Embroidery needle size 7

Cushion pad 40cm (16in) square

Dressmaker's marking pen

Fabric scissors

TO MAKE THE COVER

1 Preparing the patchwork fabric Iron all the fabric to be used and lay it out flat to avoid creasing, ready to use.

2 Arranging the patches With right sides upwards lay the patches out on a flat surface, following the diagram for the arrangement of the light and dark patches. Re-arrange the patches within the light and dark areas until you are pleased with the overall effect.

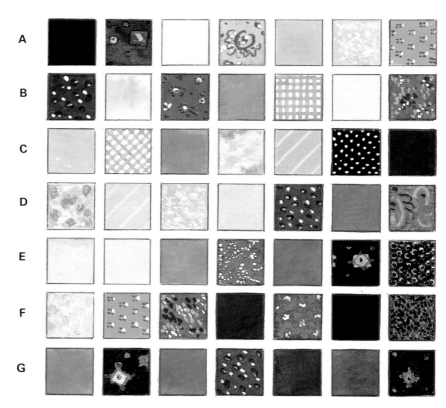

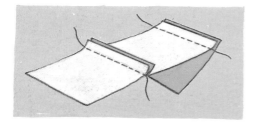

3 Stitching the patches Working along row A, taking a 1cm (⅜in) seam and with right sides facing, stitch patches A1 and A2 together. Join the opposite edge of patch A2 to A3 in the same way, then continue to join all the patches in row A in number sequence. Join rows B, C, D, E, F and G as for row A. Trim the seams. Press all the seams in rows A, C, E and G in one direction and all the seams in rows B, D and F in the opposite direction.

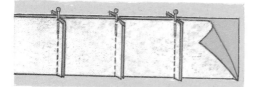

4 Joining the rows With right sides facing and aligning the seams pin rows A and B together. Using a straight stitch and taking a 1cm (⅜in) seam, sew the rows together. Join rows B, C, D, E, F and G together in the same way. Trim the seams and press to one side.

5 Making the cushion cover With right sides together, lay the patchwork on top of the backing fabric and using a straight stitch, sew a 1cm (⅜in) seam around the edge leaving a 30cm (12in) gap along one side.

6 Inserting the pad Snip the corners, then turn cover to right side and press. Insert the cushion pad and using small slip stitches, close the opening.

tip

Patch ideas
If you enjoyed making the patchwork cushion cover and feel that a quilt for your bedroom would complete the look, give it a try, you'll be surprise just how quickly the work will grow. Once finished add a border, then back and quilt the work to finish.

Stylish designer patchwork

Made in brilliant contrasting colours, a patchwork cushion adds a fresh new look to a chair. The fun of patchwork is choosing different fabrics that look good together, then arranging them for a really special design. On a grand scale, bedspreads or throws can be made to match a particular room, but experimenting with a cushion cover is a good way to learn the craft.

Materials

Medium weight patterned and plain cotton fabric 100 x 122cm (39½ x 44¼in) of each

Sewing thread to match plain fabric

Pencil, ruler and **set square**

Thick card template 7cm (2¾in) square

Craft knife

Tape measure

Fabric scissors

Press studs x 4

Chunky piping cord 2m (2¼yds)

Iron and **ironing board**

Cushion pad 40cm (16in) square

▼ Dotty appeal
Bright, freshly coloured fabrics are stitched together in simple squares to create a cushion that will bring a sunny touch to any room.

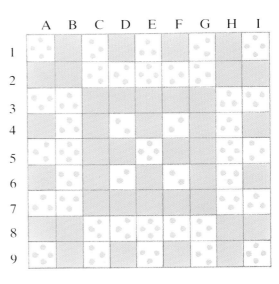

	A	B	C	D	E	F	G	H	I
1									
2									
3									
4									
5									
6									
7									
8									
9									

◄ *Play with patches*
Add a professional touch to your patchwork, by cutting out the dotty fabric paying attention to the arrangement of the dots; like dominoes.

MAKING THE COVER

1 Making the template Draw a line 1cm (³⁄₈in) inside the edges of the square card template to mark a frame. Then cut out with craft knife.

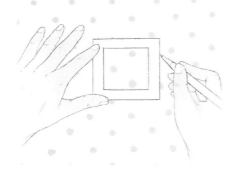

2 Cutting the patches Centre any motifs in the frame and use the template to cut 44 patterned patches and 36 plain (for this design).

3 Arranging the patches Following the layout diagram, arrange the patches on a flat surface.

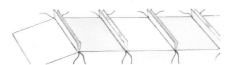

4 Stitching the patches Starting on row 1 join patches A and B along one side – with right sides facing stitch a 1cm (⁵⁄₈in) wide seam allowance – then add patches C, D, E, F and so on. Stitch remaining rows.

5 Pressing the seams Press the seams on rows 1, 3, 5, 7 and 9 in one direction, and those on rows 2, 4, 6 and 8 in the opposite direction.

6 Joining rows of patches For a good result the seams must match exactly. Stitch rows 1 and 2 with a 1cm (⁵⁄₈in) seam then join row 3 to row 2. Continue until design is complete. Press seams open.

7 Preparing the cushion back Cut two pieces of plain fabric 29 x 45cm (11½ x 17 ¾in). Turn and stitch a double hem 1cm (³⁄₈in) wide to wrong side along one long edge of both back halves. Lap one back half over the other for 9cm (3½in) so back measures 45cm (17¾in) square. Pin then tack the halves together.

8 Making the ties Cut eight lengths of printed fabric each 56 x 14cm (22 x 5½in). With wrong sides facing, fold one piece in half lengthways and trim one end at an angle. Stitch a 1cm (³⁄₈in) seam down the edge and along the angled end to make a point. Trim seam allowance on the corners; turn right side out and press. Make other ties the same.

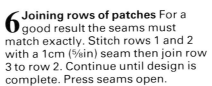

9 Covering the piping Cut four bias strips of patterned fabric 6 x 50cm (2¼ x 19¾in). With right sides facing seam short ends of strips together; press seams open. With right side outside wrap the strip lengthways around the piping cord, and using the zipper foot, stitch the strip as close to the cord as possible.

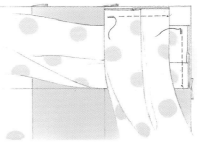

10 Positioning the ties Pleat the raw ends of each tie to a finished width of 4.5cm (1¾in). Match the side of the tie with the corner patch seam and the raw ends of both tie and patch, pin and tack.

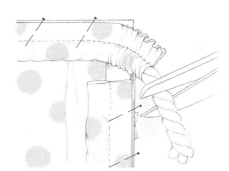

11 Positioning the piping Gently pull the casing so that it is 1.5cm (⁵⁄₈in) longer than the cord, then beginning at one corner and matching raw edges, pin piping around patchwork cushion cover. Finish piping by pushing back the casing, trimming the cord to fit end to end. Reposition casing and trim to 4cm (1¾in) longer than cord. Hand stitch the casing so that it neatly covers the cord. Tack the piping in place.

12 Completing the cover With right sides facing, pin the back to the front. Stitch a 1cm (³⁄₈in) seam around the edge close to piping cord, snip seam allowance at corners; turn right side out and press. Stitch evenly spaced press studs along back opening. Insert the cushion pad.

Patchwork lace tablecloth

The textures of satin and lace complement each other beautifully and using ready-made lace napkins. this delightful top cloth can be made quickly to transform a plain table.

If you have difficulty finding suitable square napkins. use hemmed fabric pieces of the same measurements. Whichever option you choose it is most important that the corners are truly square. or the finished top cloth will be uneven. Bows stitched to the end of each ribbon strip add the final flourish. If you want you could add extra bows to the corners of the cloth.

▲ Adding colour
The satin ribbon enhances the top cloth, highlighting the delicate lace. Try placing the top cloth over a pale tablecloth in a colour that complements the ribbon's colour. Plain and patterned cloths work well.

Materials

Square lace napkins four × 48cm (19in) square

Double sided satin ribbon 5cm (2in) wide × 6.5m (7¼ft)

Fusible webbing (Wundaweb) 2.5cm (1in) wide x 2.25m (3ft 6in) long

Sewing thread to match ribbon

Embroidery needle size 7

Iron and **ironing board**

Pressing cloth

Ruler and **pins**

MAKING THE TABLECLOTH

1 Preparing the napkins Press the napkins to remove any creases. Check the napkin corners are square and if they are not, use other suitable napkins to ensure a flat tablecloth.

2 Preparing the ribbon Cut two lengths of ribbon each measuring 110cm (43½in). Fold one length in half lengthways and widthways, then tack a line of stitches along the folds. Work second ribbon length as for first.

3 Positioning the Wundaweb Cut the Wundaweb in half lengthways, then cut one strip 48cm (19in) long. Lay the ribbon flat on the ironing board and position the short strip of Wundaweb on the ribbon, 6mm (⅜in) from the tacking stitches.

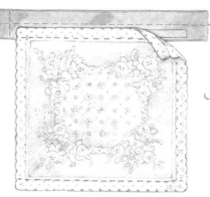

4 Attaching one napkin With the wrong side downwards, lay napkin over Wundaweb positioning edges 6mm (⅜in) from the tacked lines. Make sure that the Wundaweb is along the edge of the hem, then use a damp pressing cloth and warm iron to press in place. Turn work over and use a warm dry iron to press the ribbon securely in place.

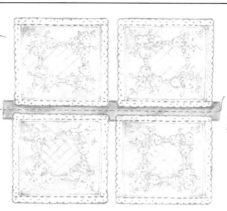

5 Attaching the remaining napkins Cut three more narrow Wundaweb strips each 48cm (19in) long and using the tacking stitches as a guide, fix the remaining three napkins in place along the ribbon as before.

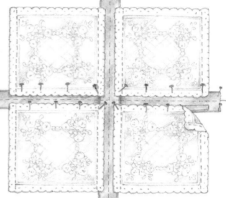

6 Joining the last piece of ribbon Lay the second ribbon on the ironing board and place the cloth over it so the ribbon fills the gap. Line up the napkin 6mm (⅜in) from the tacking stitches and pin to the board to prevent slipping. Tuck the Wundaweb between the ribbon and napkins, then iron.

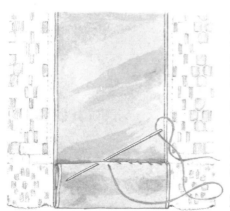

7 Neatening the ribbon ends Trim ribbon ends to within 5cm (2in) of napkin hems, then fold the ribbon to the wrong side with a double hem so that it is level with the napkin hems. Press ribbon hem and taking care that stitches do not show on the right side of the work, use tiny slip stitches to sew hem into place.

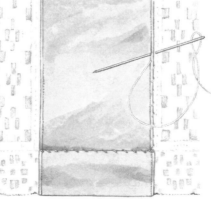

8 Stitching the napkins If the cloth is to be used and washed frequently it is a good idea to stitch the ribbon and napkins together using tiny slip stitches on wrong side of the work.

9 Fixing the bows in place Cut the last ribbon into four equal lengths and tie each to form a bow. Trim the ends and stitch each bow to a ribbon end, between two napkins.

tip

Sew easy
If you have access to a sewing machine, stitch the cloth with small machine stitches. Check for pucker by machine stitching a double thickness of ribbon before sewing the cloth.

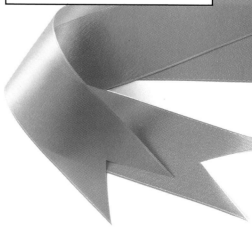

Cut-through appliqué

Cut-through, or reverse appliqué is worked by cutting away areas from a top layer of fabric to reveal a contrast colour beneath. The fabric layers can be padded, lined and quilted, so the technique is ideal for working home accessories like the comfortable throw and matching cushion design.

Simple geometric patterns are the easiest to sew and these, worked in contrast colours create striking effects. Choose natural fibre fabrics such as light to midweight cotton for reverse appliqué, as this handles well. The cut edges of the design are turned in and handstitched, so you need a non-slippery fabric which does not fray easily. Dark colours can be worked over lighter shades, and vice versa; but if using a light top colour like we have, make sure the fabric is dense enough to prevent the darker under-layer from showing through.

▼ Casual comfort
Bold contrasting colours effectively display the simple geometric shapes of this wonderful throw, which has been worked using the technique of cut-through appliqué.

1sq = 5cm

◄ *Geometric border*
The border pattern is used for both the throw and the cushion. Scale it up on dressmaker's graph paper, and use the pattern, repeating it as necessary, to fit around the edge of the throw. For the cushion use the corner piece as the centre, and edge with the inner motif.

The throw
Finished size 146cm (57½in) square.

Materials
Unbleached cotton fabric For the top and base layer you will need 3m (3⅜yd) of 150cm (60in) wide cotton fabric in cream, or another light-coloured but dense cotton fabric
Contrast cotton fabric 1.90m (2⅛yd) of 150cm (60in) wide lightweight cotton in terracotta, or your chosen appliqué colour
Domette 1.50m (1⅝yd) of 140cm (55in) wide domette for interlining
Embroidery cotton Stranded thread for central quilting, to match the contrasting fabric
Sewing threads to match throw colours
Embroidery scissors
Dressmaker's metric graph paper
Wad punch or **bradawl**
Pencil
Ruler
Water or **air erasable dressmaker's marker pen**

MAKING THE THROW

1 Transferring the pattern Scale up the design from the diagram on to dressmaker's graph paper. Punch a hole in the paper pattern at each corner point of the design using a wad punch or bradawl.

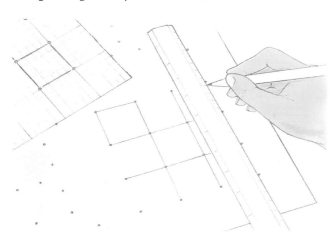

2 Marking design Cut a 145cm (57in) square from the cream, top layer fabric (A). Lay paper pattern over, lining up all edges. Transfer the design on to the fabric by marking dots through the punched holes with a pencil. Remove pattern, and join up the dots with ruler and pencil. Mark the corner sections first, then repeat the design once more to join the corner sections.

3 Adding layers Cut a 145cm (57in) square of terracotta cotton (B), and cut away an 80cm (31½in) square from the centre. Cut another 145cm (57in) square from cream fabric (D), and a 145cm (57in) length of domette (C). Lay (D) fabric flat with wrong side facing upwards, and centre the domette (C) on top. Place contrast fabric (B) over this with right side upwards. Tack the layers together round the inner edge of the contrast fabric.

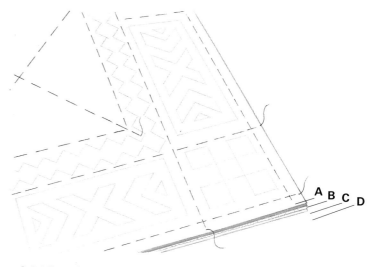

A B C D

4 Adding the top layer With right side facing upwards, lay the pattern-marked fabric (A) over the others, and tack through all layers.

5 Working the diamond border Starting on the inner edge of the border, and within the outline of the diamond, carefully cut a small hole through the top layer of fabric (A). Cut a turning allowance of 6mm (¼in), parallel to the drawn line. Snip into this allowance at corner points to ease the fabric around the corners. Turn the fabric under along the drawn line, pin the turnings in place and secure them with very small stitches and matching thread. Repeat with the opposite edge of the diamond border.

▲ *Checkered corner*
The repeat pattern.

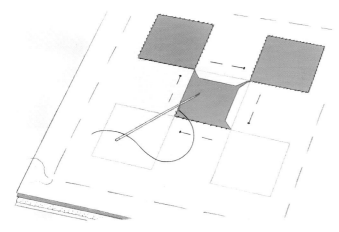

6 Checkered motifs Cut and stitch the eight checkered motifs in the same way, allowing 6mm (¼in) for turnings. Work one square at a time to prevent fraying.

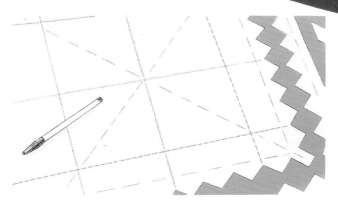

8 Quilting lines Using the erasable marker pen, mark the quilting lines on the top fabric (A). With stranded cotton work 6mm (¼in) evenly spaced quilting stitches across these lines.

9 Binding the edges Cut two 145 x 10cm (57 x 4in) and two 148 x 10cm (58½ x 4in) strips of terracotta fabric. With throw right side up, pin and machine stitch a shorter strip to one side (right sides facing) with a 2.5cm (1in) turning. Turn under 2.5cm (1in) and handsew binding strip to wrong side to cover machine stitching.

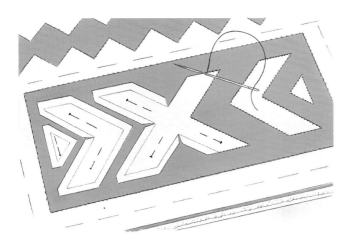

7 Rectangular panel motifs First pin the inner sections of the design in place before you begin cutting and stitching the main outer sides. Cut round the pinned pieces allowing 6mm (¼in) for turnings. Turn edges in and stitch in place.

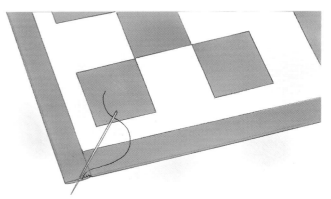

10 Completing the throw Repeat on the opposite side of the throw, then bind the two remaining sides in the same way, using the longer terracotta strips. Fold under and handsew the excess 1.5cm (⅝in) at each end. Remove all the tacking stitches.

▲ **Checkered cushion** *The rustic brown and cream of the matching cushion merges easily into a country interior.*

The cushion
Made using the same fabric and design as the throw, this cushion cover is just as decorative on its own. The finished cover size is 40cm (16in) square.

Materials
Fabrics; 50cm (⅝yd) or 150cm (60in) **wide unbleached cotton** or another light, but dense colour. 50cm (⅝yd) of 150cm (60in) **wide contrast cotton** (if you have made the throw, you could use the 80cm (31½in) square that was cut from the centre of the terracotta contrast fabric), and 50cm (⅝yd) of 140cm (55in) **wide domette**
Nylon zip 30cm (12in) midweight zip for insertion in the back of the cushion cover in a similar shade to the main cushion fabric
Matching sewing threads as listed for the throw
Stranded embroidery thread to match the contrasting fabric as listed for the throw
Cushion pad, 35cm (14in) square
Design and **sewing aids** as listed for the throw

MAKING THE CUSHION

1 Transferring the design Cut a 40cm (16in) square of cream top fabric (A) and transfer the checkered motif to the centre. Surround with the diamond border, leaving a 1.5cm (⅝in) gap between the motif and the border.

2 Working the design Cut one more 40cm (16in) square of cream fabric (D), one 40cm (16in) square of contrast fabric (B) and one of domette (C). Layer these in the same formation as for the throw, with (A) on top, and work appliqué as before.

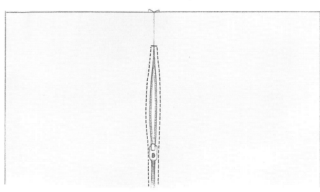

3 Cushion back Cut two 40 x 21.5cm (16 x 8½in) pieces of cream fabric. Taking a 1.5cm (⅝in) seam allowance, stitch together 5cm (2in) in from each end on one long side. Press seam open, and insert zip.

4 Finishing cushion Pin the zipped back piece to the appliquéd front piece, with wrong sides facing. Cut two 40 x 10cm (16 x 4in) and two 43 x 10cm (17 x 4in) strips from contrast colour (B), and bind the cushion edges as for the throw, starting with the shorter strips.

Joining domette
If the domette is not the required width, join a strip to one side to make up the difference. Overlap the two edges very slightly, and join them by working an evenly spaced herringbone stitch through both layers taking care not to pull the stitches tightly.

Loose chair covers

Even the most basic wooden, wicker or plastic chair can be transformed into a stunning piece of furniture with the addition of a loosely tailored cover. These fabric covers are perfect for disguising worn or damaged chairs and sofas, and allow you to give these a completely new look, in half the time and expense involved in re-upholstery. If you have young children or pets about your home, fitted fabric covers are also the ideal way to protect a favourite chair from daily wear and tear; should the cover become damaged, it can easily be removed for repair and cleaning.

The covers are only partially fitted and hang loosely over the chairs, so that the chairs' contours are clearly outlined, but are given a far softer look. Make the fabric covers as simple or complicated as you like, depending on how tailored a look you are aiming for. By using several pieces of fabric, stitched together along the chairs' edges, you can achieve a perfect fit. Alternatively, simply use one or two pieces of fabric draped over a chair for a looser fit; excess fabric can then be gathered or pleated into soft folds, held in place with matching decorative ties or bows.

▼ **Simple stripes**
A striped fabric makes a stylish but informal loose cover, which will complement a simple, uncluttered setting perfectly.

Suitable fabrics

Choose a hardwearing fabric which is fairly crease-resistant, but also one that drapes well into soft folds or pleats. A tough furnishing cotton, hardwearing ticking or linen union are all ideal. Make sure the fabric is washable, and wash it before making the cover to avoid shrinkage afterwards.

Patterned fabrics, stripes and plains can all look equally effective if the style and colour are chosen with the setting in mind. Use decorative bows and ties, in matching or contrasting shades, to keep folds and gathers in place.

▶ Before and after

This plain wicker chair is given a softer, more comfortable look with a loosely tailored cover. Make the decorative ties in the same fabric as the cover, as here, or use a plain fabric in a toning colour to emphasize them as design details.

FITTED CHAIR COVER

This chair cover is made up from eight pieces of fabric, for a perfectly tailored look. The cover slips easily over the chair with the aid of two inverted pleats, one behind each back leg, which are held in place with decorative bow ties; two bows at the front of the chair balance the design and soften its tailored lines.

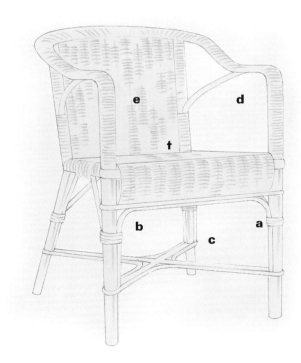

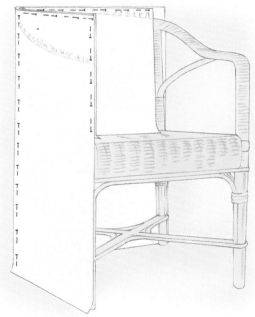

1 Measuring up Draw a rough plan of the chair, and mark on the measurements of each section. Use a tape measure to measure each section of the chair, taking the measurement at the broadest point across its width and length; measure the outer sections first – the exterior arms (**a**), the outer back (**b**) and the lower front panel (**c**), all floor length; then the inner ones – the interior arms (**d**) and the inside back (**e**), both to the seat only; and finally the seat (**f**).

2 Making a pattern From paper (or an old sheet), cut out eight rectangles to fit the chair's measurements, plus 3cm (1¼in) all round. Hold the paper pieces against the appropriate parts of the chair and pin them together, 3cm (1¼in) in from their edges; begin by pinning the outer panels to the inner ones along the top edges, then join the side edges. Pinch-fold them over any curves and use a pencil to trace along these lines, so that the chair's contours are marked clearly on the paper pattern. Remove each pattern piece. Cut around any curves marked, adding a 3cm (1¼in) allowance.

3 Cutting out Lay the fabric out flat, right side up, and pin the pattern pieces to it. Use tailor's chalk to trace the pattern on to the fabric. If using a patterned fabric, try to arrange the pattern pieces so that any motifs are centred and the fabric matches across the seams – this takes longer and requires more fabric, but gives a more professional finish. Cut out each fabric piece. Also cut out two gusset strips for the pleats, the height of the chair back and 13cm (5¼in) wide.

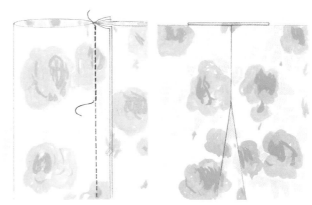

6 Forming the inverted pleats With right sides facing, fold one gusset strip in half lengthways, so that the two seam lines lie on top of each other. Stitch over the seam lines, from the top of each pleat down towards the bottom for 8-10cm (3¼-4in), to hold the pleats in place. Then open out the fabric panels and centre the gusset strip behind them; press in place.

7 Stitching the cover Re-pin the outer panels to the inner ones and stitch all the sections together. Press the seams flat and turn the cover right side out.

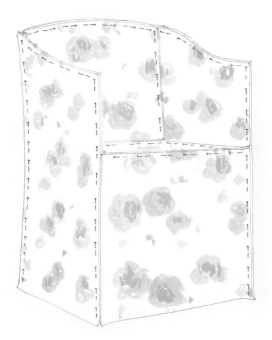

8 Hemming the cover Place the cover over the chair, making sure it lies straight. Turn under and pin a double hem around the bottom edge of the chair cover, so that the fabric just rests on the floor, or lies just above it; make sure the hemline is straight across the pleats. Remove the cover from the chair and stitch the hem; trim the fabric a little to neaten before stitching, if you find it is very uneven.

9 Making the ties From your chosen fabric, cut out four strips measuring 10 x 35cm (4 x 14in) and two strips measuring 10 x 50cm (4 x 19¾in). Fold one strip in half lengthways, right sides facing. Stitch down the unfolded long edge of the strip and across one short edge, taking a 1cm (⅜in) seam allowance. Turn through to right side, turn in raw ends of strip and slip-stitch to close. Press to flatten. Repeat with the other fabric strips to make six ties – two long and four short.

4 Checking the fit With right sides facing, pin the fabric sections together (except the gusset strips), pinning 3cm (1¼in) in from the edges. Place the cover inside out over the chair to check the fit; move the pins to make adjustments, if necessary. Once you are fully satisfied with the fit, unpin the back corner seams to remove the cover from the chair. Trim all the seam allowances to 1.5cm (⅝in).

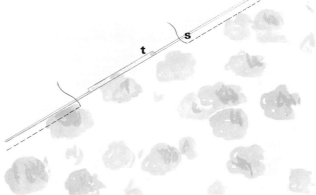

5 Attaching the gusset strips With right sides facing and allowing a 1.5cm (⅝in) seam allowance, pin and stitch a gusset strip down one side of the outer back panel; then pin and stitch the other side of the strip to the edge of the outer side panel. Attach the second gusset strip to the other side of the back panel in the same way. You will find this easier if you temporarily unpin the inner chair sections from the outer ones. Trim the tops of the strips so that they are in line with the panels, if necessary.

10 Attaching the ties Halfway down one gusset side seam (**s**), unpick a 5.5cm (2¼in) length of stitching. Insert the end of one short tie (**t**) by 1.5cm (⅝in), then stitch the seam together again to anchor the tie. Attach the other short ties in the same way, one to the other gusset side seam, and two halfway down each gusset back seam. Tie the two long ties into bows and slipstitch these to the front corners of the cover, where the seat meets the arms. Slip the cover over the chair and tie the back ties into bows to hold the pleats in place.

QUICK IDEAS

A range of loosely tailored chair and sofa covers can be made from only one or two sheets of fabric, carefully draped, tucked and secured with a few stitches.

Draped cover A delightful cover for an old armchair, shown right, is made from a large piece of fabric or a *grande voile*. Drape it loosely over the chair, tucking it in around the seat, for a comfortable, informal look.

▼ *Folded to fit*
With a few well-placed tucks, a single sheet of fabric can be transformed into a stylish cover.

▶ *Decorative feature*
Bunch up any excess fabric around a ball of tissue paper, and secure it with matching tassels.

Single piece cover The sofa cover shown left is made from a single sheet of fabric, tucked and draped at key points. Arrange the sheet on the sofa. Make a tuck halfway across the seat to give the impression of two cushion pads and to create a soft fold at the front. Then tuck any excess fabric between the seat and both sofa arms until the fabric rests on the floor at each side. Finally, tuck the fabric underneath the seat along the sofa back and front to lift the front and back fabric edges to the correct length. Drape the fabric around the sofa arms in loose folds, and hold these in place with matching or contrasting bows, slip-stitched over the folds.

Loose sofa cover The loosely fitted sofa cover shown right is made from three main pieces of fabric – one to cover the middle section and two for the arms. To make the wide middle section, simply join fabric widths together, matching the pattern across the seams. The two arm pieces are gathered up along the top seam before being joined to the main piece, so that they fall in soft, loose folds; cut the fabric for the arms half as wide again as the actual arm measurement to allow for the gathering. Hold the cover in place with matching fabric ties.

▶ *Playing with stripes*
If using a striped fabric, aim for a lively effect by placing each section at right angles to its neighbour.

Braids and tassels

Silky ropes and tassels catch the light and add lustre to rich, high gloss fabrics. For a less formal look, choose braids and trimmings made of heavy cotton, in more muted colours so their effect is more homely and cottage-like. If you decide to trim one item in a room – curtains, for example – why not extend the theme elsewhere, on to the sofa cushions. By repeating an interesting detail, you will give the room unity.

If possible, take a sample of the base fabric along with you when you are choosing trimmings. For the best visual results it's usually safer to aim for an interesting contrast rather than a perfect match. Many of the heavier home furnishing trimmings require dry cleaning, while trimmings designed for clothes are more likely to be hand washable. Before applying cotton trimmings, pre-shrink them by soaking in hot water for ten minutes. Dry on a towel and press with the right side down on the towel to avoid flattening the texture of the braid.

▲ Needlework pastimes
Tapestry designs are ideal for making up into decorative cushions. To give them a real 'heirloom' finish use cords and tassels in colours picked out from the design.

tip

Frayed ends
Silky braids tend to unwind or fray easily. To prevent this happening while working with them, bind the cut ends with adhesive tape which is trimmed off when you are ready to finish the trimming.

◀ **Grand tassels**
The rich red in the floral pattern on these textured curtains is highlighted by the opulent rope and tasselled trimming and tiebacks. The thick cord is knotted at every pleat on the curtain heading and then tied in a bow where the curtains meet. The ends are finished off with big, bold tassels.

▼ **Rustic charm**
This softly fluttering macramé fringe makes an instant valance for a cottage window. To re-create the idea in your own home use deep purchased braid or look for old trimmings in junk shops.

▼ **Unusual handles**
Large chunky tassels, with crocheted bases, make an interesting alternative to knobs on this wooden cabinet.

Lace flourishes

Cotton lace panels and lace table-cloths can be used in various ways to add a quick lift to soft furnishings. You may have odd lengths left over from curtain making or old curtains which did not fit the windows when you moved house, and which you were reluctant to throw away. These ideas require the minimum of sewing – in fact some need no sewing at all.

▼ **Flounces and frills** For the festoon cloth (left), stitch short lengths of transparent festoon blind tape at intervals round the edge of the cloth and at right angles to it. The distance between the tapes will depend on the kind of the flounce you want – shallow curves will need short lengths of tape set quite wide apart, while deeper curves use longer pieces of tape set closer

together. Stitch up the centre of each tape, knot the cords at one end then pull up cords to gather and knot to hold.

The frilled cloth (right) is a small circular cloth which has been enlarged by the addition of a frill made from a similar lace. Deep lace frills with a finished edge are sold in the soft furnishing section of large department stores.

◄ Quick cushion covers
Lengths of lace panelling can be wrapped round plain coloured cushions and seamed together across the back. To hold the cover in place, simply tie the sides together with a couple of ribbon bows which match the original cushion.

▼ Tied up with bows An attractive lace panel has been tied with grosgrain ribbon to a brass curtain pole to make a permanent curtain over a small window. Or use this idea to add a lace finish to a brass bedhead.

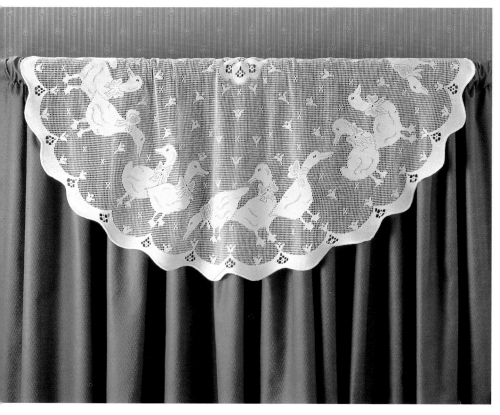

◄ Tablecloth curtain valance A circular lace cloth draped over a curtain pole becomes an original valance – also a good way of giving a damaged or stained cloth a new lease of life. Use it on a window where the curtains are tied back at the sides during the day.

Adding bows

The supple, flowing shape of fabric bows gives a lift to soft furnishings and other decorative items around the home, drawing attention to a particular feature or providing the focal point themselves. Use them on pelmets and valances, cushions, tablecloths, chair covers and for a host of other decorative applications.

To give neutral furnishings vitality, attach bows in warm or vibrant colours, and add touches of the same colour elsewhere in the room. Where the furnishings don't quite co-ordinate, use the bows as a link, adding them for example, to the window dressing to tie in with a contrasting sofa.

The bows can be made in one or more pieces, producing a more tailored look the more pieces used. For a dramatic or formal effect they can be starched, interfaced or padded with wadding to give them more body and to hold their shape. For a softer, more informal look, a length of lightweight fabric such as chiffon or a piece of satin

▲ Double delight
Simple double bows like these are easy to make and can have a major impact on the decorative scheme of the room. Here, they are made in a pretty blue and white fabric to tie in with the china and chair seats.

ribbon can be tied into a soft, floppy bow. The fabric and setting will usually dictate whether a grand, tailored bow is best or something more soft and simple.

DECORATIVE BOW

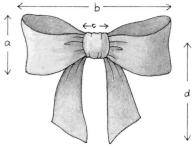

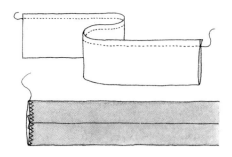

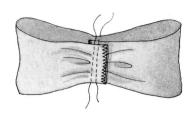

1 Cutting out For the loops, cut out a piece of fabric twice the finished depth **(a)** by twice the finished width **(b)** of the bow, adding 1cm (⅜in) seam allowances all round. For the tails, cut two pieces of fabric the finished width of each tail by twice the finished length from the centre of the knot to the tip **(d)**, adding 1cm (⅜in) seam allowances all round. For the knot, cut a piece of fabric twice the finished width **(c)** by 13cm (5in), adding 1cm (⅜in) seam allowances all round.

2 Making loops and knot Fold the loop fabric in half with right sides facing so that the long edges match. Pin and then stitch the long raw edges together, taking a 1cm (⅜in) seam allowance. Open out the fabric and position the seam at the centre; press with seam allowances open, then turn right side out. Repeat to stitch the knot piece. Neaten the raw edges of both the loop and knot with overlock or zigzag.

3 Finishing the loops With the seam on top, fold the ends over to the middle, overlapping by 2cm (¾in). Run two rows of gathering stitches up the centre of the overlap, taking the stitches through all layers. Gather up and knot the threads to secure.

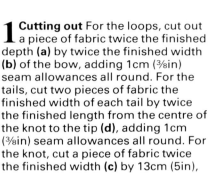

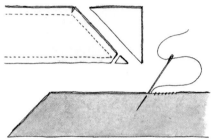

4 Preparing the tail pieces Pin or tack the tail pieces together all round with raw edges matching and right sides facing. To shape the ends, either turn the fabric up at each end so that the end is level with one long edge, or fold in half lengthways and then turn each end up so it is level with the raw side edges. Unfold the fabric and draw along the foldlines with tailor's chalk.

5 Stitching the tails Stitch the tail pieces together all round, taking a 1cm (⅜in) seam allowance and stitching 1cm (⅜in) inside the chalk line at each end; leave a 10cm (4in) gap in the centre of one long edge to turn through. Trim the excess fabric at the ends, and snip to, but not through the stitching at the points. Turn right side out through the gap, then neatly slipstitch the gap closed.

6 Attaching the tails Run two rows of gathering stitches up the centre of the tail piece and gather up to the same width as the centre of the bow. Place the loop piece face down and centre the tail piece on top, then stitch together along the centre to hold, using a double thread. Don't worry about the stitches showing on the front – these will be covered by the knot piece.

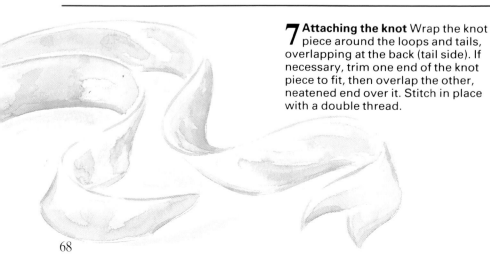

7 Attaching the knot Wrap the knot piece around the loops and tails, overlapping at the back (tail side). If necessary, trim one end of the knot piece to fit, then overlap the other, neatened end over it. Stitch in place with a double thread.

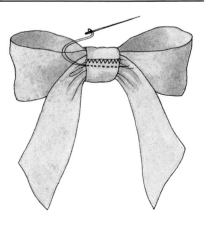

SOFT DOUBLE BOW

This is a soft decorative bow which has two loop pieces instead of one. The loops should be cut slightly longer than the finished size because they are opened out like the petals of a flower in the finished bow, making them appear slightly smaller.

Making the double bow Cut out the fabric (see step 1 for a decorative bow) but cut two loops instead of one. Make up the bow pieces following steps 2-5 for a decorative bow, but omitting the gathering stitches on the loops. Place one finished loop on top of the other, and place both centrally on top of the tails. Wrap the knot round all three pieces and pin at the back. Open out the loops and arrange as required. Carefully trim away the excess knot fabric at the back, then stitch firmly to hold, catching the loops in the stitching to secure.

PADDED BOW

A light padding of polyester wadding will give a decorative bow extra body and shape. Use a padded bow where you want it to create maximum impact. For a crisp look, without the extra bulk of wadding, interfacing can be used instead, ironed on to the wrong side of the fabric pieces.

1 Cutting out Carefully cut out the main fabric as for step 1 of a decorative bow. For the loops, cut a piece of light or mediumweight wadding the finished depth of the loops plus 1cm (⅜in), by twice the finished length plus 2cm (¾in). For the tails, cut a piece of wadding exactly the same size as one of the fabric tails.

▲ Functional bows
Decorative bows in pink and blue add character to the tea table and chairs. Both sets are functional – securing the cushions and covering the gathers on the cloth.

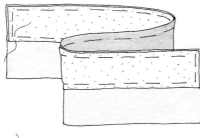

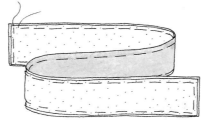

2 Making the bow Tack the wadding to the wrong side of the loop piece, level with one long edge. Tack the remaining piece of wadding to the wrong side of one tail piece. Make up the bow, following the instructions for a decorative bow following the steps 2-7, and trimming the excess wadding at the seam allowances to reduce bulk.

tip

Right direction
If the tails of the decorative bow are long and the fabric has an obvious direction, cut them in four pieces the finished width by the finished length of each tail, adding 1cm (⅜in) seam allowances all round. Join together at the centre with the pattern pointing to the seam. This way the pattern will run vertically in the bow.

TAILORED DOUBLE BOW

A tailored double bow is an elegant variation of a decorative bow, and more formal than the soft double bow. It has two pressed loops, with the top one slightly smaller than the bottom one. The tails can either be positioned behind, as in a standard tailored bow, or folded and stitched to the back to create a T-shaped bow, as pictured above.

1 Cutting out Cut out the fabric as for step 1 of a decorative bow, but cut two loop pieces instead of one. Cut the top loop piece 2-4cm (¾-1½in) shorter than the lower loop so that it will sit neatly on top of the lower loop piece. Now proceed as follows for either style:

▲ **T-time**
A T-shaped tailored bow adds elegance to an unusual gathered cushion and covers the join where the gathered fabric meets.

2 Standard tailored bow Make up the bow following the instructions for a decorative bow, steps 2-5. Run two rows of gathering stitches up the centre of the tail piece to gather to the same depth as the loops. Centre the smaller loop piece on top of the larger one and then centre the tails behind both. Pin and then stitch together at the centre using a double thread. Wrap the knot piece round the centre of the bow, overlapping at the back and stitch.

3 T-shaped bow Make up the bow pieces as for a decorative bow, steps 2-5. Centre the smaller loop over the larger one and stitch together at the centre. Wrap the knot around the bow and stitch at the back, trimming away excess fabric. Run two rows of gathering stitches up the centre of the tail piece and gather up to the depth of the loops. Fold in half widthways, and pin to the back of the bow. Arrange for a pleasing effect, then stitch.

Picture bows

Pretty picture bows are cleverly designed to give the illusion of holding up the picture, but actually serve a purely decorative function. Use them to add interest to a plain picture frame and to soften its hard lines, or to fill empty wall space around the picture.

The bows are hung on a small hook placed just above the picture, which is then hung in the usual way to cover the tails of the bow. If you choose a style with long tails which extend below the picture – perhaps to provide a decorative

link with a second picture directly below the first – simply thread the tails through the picture wire to lie against the back of the picture.

The size of the bow should be chosen in accordance with the picture size, but 18cm (7in) across and 7.5cm (3in) deep is a good average size to work to. Be sure not to make your bows too small and insignificant, or too dominant in size and colour – they should provide decorative detail without detracting from the picture. Relatively stiff fabrics with a

slight sheen to them, such as moiré and slubbed silk, work well and make luxurious bows. If using a fine fabric, stiffen it with interlining for a fuller, more shapely bow.

▼ Picture this
A picture bow made from a fabric whose colour and pattern is echoed in other soft furnishings throughout the room, provides a pleasing link between the picture and its surroundings.

Materials

Fabric for making the bow
Tailor's chalk
Matching sewing threads
Two curtain weights for the tails
Small curtain ring for hanging the bow

MAKING A PICTURE BOW

For a perfectly symmetrical shape and neat finish, picture bows are often made up from three separate sections of fabric stitched together, rather than from a single continuous strip. Before you begin, decide on a good size for your bow in relation to the picture, and on a suitable length for the tails.

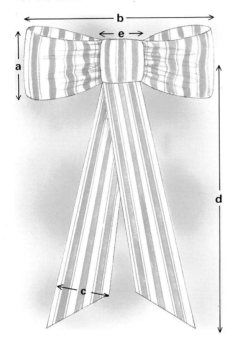

1 Cutting out For the loops of the bow, cut out a strip of fabric twice the depth of the finished bow not including tails (**a**), by twice its width (**b**). For the tails, cut out a strip of fabric twice the width of each finished tail (**c**) by twice the length from the centre of the knot to the tail tip (**d**). For the knot, cut a piece of fabric twice the width of the finished knot (**e**), by 12cm (4¾in). Add a 1cm (⅜in) seam allowance all round each piece. Cut out along the straight grain.

2 Stitching the loops With right sides together, fold the strip of fabric for the loop in half lengthways. Taking a 1cm (⅜in) seam allowance, pin and stitch along the long raw edges and across one short edge. Turn the strip through to the right side and press, keeping the seam on the lower edge. Turn in the raw ends and slipstitch to close, then stitch the two short ends of the strip together to form a loop.

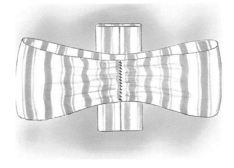

3 Forming the bow Fold and stitch the long edges of the fabric strip for the knot in same way, centre the seam, then stitch across one short edge. Turn through to right side. With the seamed side against the loop, wrap the knot piece around the centre, so that it pulls the loop in to form a bow. Trim raw end of knot piece if it is too long, then turn in the raw edges and slipstitch ends of knot piece together. Then stitch in place on back of bow.

▲ **Pretty as a picture**
Depending on the choice of fabric, picture bows can look as informal or sophisticated as you like. The colourful striped fabric shown here makes a wonderfully fresh bow, ideal for both the natural image of the picture and its simple setting.

4 Shaping the tails With right sides facing, fold the strip of fabric for the tails in half lengthways and pin together around the raw edges. The ends of the strip are decoratively shaped into two points. At one end of the strip, use tailor's chalk to mark a diagonal line from the raw-edged corner to the long folded edge opposite, and repeat at the other end, from the folded corner to the long raw edge opposite.

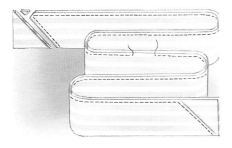

5 **Stitching the tails** Taking a 1cm (⅜in) seam allowance, stitch along the strip and across both shaped ends, leaving a small gap in the long edge for turning through. Trim excess fabric at both ends and snip into corners, then turn through to right side. Insert a curtain weight at each end, and slipstitch the opening to close. Press to lie flat.

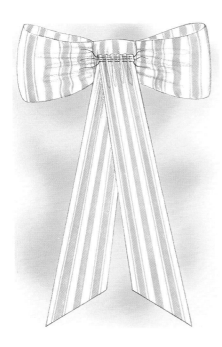

6 **Attaching the tails** Fold the tail strip in half widthways, with the pointed tips at the end of the strip facing outwards; fold at a slight angle so that the two tails spread out along their length. Run two rows of gathering threads across the folded top edge of the tails, and gather up slightly to fit the width of the knot. Secure the threads, then stitch the tails to the knot at the back of the bow.

7 **Hanging the bow** Stitch the small curtain ring to the back of the knot at the centre of the bow; quickly check that the ring is not visible from the front of the bow before you stitch it in place. Hang the bow in position on a picture hook just above your picture. Then hang the picture on its hook below the bow, slipping the tails of the bow through the picture wire to lie against the back of the picture close to the wall.

FULL PICTURE BOW

The style of a picture bow can easily be varied to suit not only the picture, but also the setting. The design featured here is a stunning way to display a picture in a room with a picture rail, by means of a full bow attached to a long, slim fabric strip. Before you begin, hang the picture in place as usual.

1 **Cutting out** Cut out fabric pieces for the loops, knot and tails of the bow as described in step 1 of *Making a picture bow*, but note that the tails are kept quite short in this design. For 'hanging' the picture, also cut a strip of fabric 18cm (7in) wide, by the distance from the picture rail to the top of your picture plus 10cm (4in) in length.

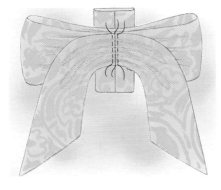

2 **Making up the bow** Make up loops and knot as before, but do not join them together. Stitch tail strip, shaping ends, but mark one diagonal in opposite direction to other; do not insert weights. Run two rows of gathering stitches across centre of tail piece, and gather up slightly. Centre tail piece over join on loops of bow, and stitch in place. Wrap the knot piece around the loops and tails, and stitch in position.

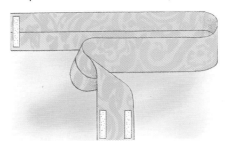

3 **Stitching the hanging strip** Fold and stitch the hanging strip as for the loops, but centring the seam. Sew the stitching half of a length of Sew 'n' Stick Velcro across the top of the strip, on the wrong side, and stick the other half in place on the picture rail ridge. Stitch two lengths of Velcro vertically to lower end of strip, on the right side, and attach a horizontal Velcro strip centrally across top of picture back.

4 **Hanging the picture** Run two rows of gathering stitches across the hanging strip, where the bow will be positioned, and gather the strip up slightly. Stitch the bow in position over the gathered part of the strip, to give the impression that the bow is tied around it. Match the Velcro strips to fix the hanging strip to the picture rail, and to the back of the picture. The strip should lie taut as if holding up the picture – the Velcro will allow you to make adjustments as necessary.

▲ *Hanging high*
This unusual picture bow puts the room's picture rail to decorative use, and draws the eye to the attractive border beneath it. The fullness of the bow counterbalances the wide picture perfectly.

tip

Paper bows
A stylish picture bow can quickly be made from a length of crêpe paper ribbon. Simply tie a loose knot halfway along the crêpe paper strip, and slip first one, then the other end of the strip under and through the front of the knot to form a bow. Tighten by pulling on the back of the bow, and adjust until symmetrical, then glue or staple the tails in place.

Fabric frame-ups

A plain clip-on picture frame can be given a touch of country charm with the addition of a frilled fabric surround. Like picture bows, the frilled trim will serve to soften the hard outline of the frame, give it added interest and highlight the picture. Use a fairly stiff fabric to make the trim, and keep to relatively subdued colours and patterns, which will not draw attention away from the picture.

Materials

Clip-on picture frame, to include **hardboard backing, glass front, white mounting card** and **metal clips**; use a suitable size for your picture

Fabric for the frilled surround – a stiff cotton is ideal; you will need a rectangle of fabric 10.5cm (4in) larger than the frame all round

Iron-on interfacing the same size as the fabric

Spray adhesive

Rubber-solution adhesive

Pinking shears and **matching threads**

▼ Frilled frames

Frilled fabric borders give a soft touch to the hard lines of a plain glass frame, and really draw attention to the picture they surround. Keep to pretty but subtle fabrics for the best results.

MAKING THE FRAME

1 Cutting out Iron the interfacing on to the back of your fabric rectangle, then carefully trim around the edges with pinking shears. Lay the fabric out flat and centre the frame over it. Draw around the frame on to the fabric, then cut away the middle of the fabric rectangle to leave a border.

2 Sticking the border in place Lay out the hardboard backing, inner side up, and pencil a line 1cm (⅜in) in from the edges all round – this will help you achieve a straight border. Place the fabric border, right side up, around the hardboard. Glue the top corners in place on the pencil line, and gather up the inside border edge to fit the width of the frame; glue the border in place across the top edge of the hardboard backing, taking the pencilled line as your guide. Then stick the two bottom corners in place and gather up rest of border. Only a few gathers are necessary to create the effect and avoid the border becoming too bulky.

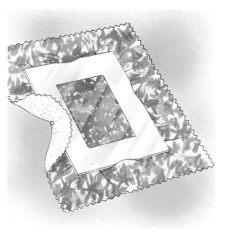

3 Assembling the frame Use the spray adhesive to mount your picture centrally on white card, then place it over the backing board to enclose glued frill edges. Lie glass panel over picture. Clip frame together, carrying the fabric frill forward over the glass with the clips, and then pulling it back outwards to conceal them. Hang picture as usual.

Stylish rosettes

Rosettes are a delightful addition to the country home, adding style and character to pelmets, tiebacks, bed canopies, and many other soft furnishings. In their many handsome forms, they make an attractive alternative to decorative bows, or can be combined with bows in co-ordinated colours or fabrics for a really elegant and sumptuous arrangement.

Like fabric bows, rosettes can be used to highlight a particular feature, to provide added decorative interest, or to cover up gathering stitches or joins in soft furnishings. They are particularly effective on swag and tail arrangements, where they can be used to emphasize the shape of the decoration and to cover the joins or the fixtures.

For the most formal effect, make a pleated rosette in a tartan, striped fabric or elegant mini-print with a co-ordinated covered button at the centre. For a softer effect, choose the simple, but attractive Maltese cross style and combine it with soft fabric bows in the same fabrics. For the softest effect of all, opt for the puff-ball rosette, in a plain or subtle fabric design which emphasizes the soft folds of the cloth.

▲ Bedroom splendour
Splendid double rosettes in the pleated style define the shape of these suptuous bed drapes. The cream fabric on the rosettes, which matches the lining of the drapes, creates a border effect and adds extra body to make the rosettes look all the more soft and luxurious.

Materials for all rosettes
Furnishing fabric for the main part of the rosette and to cover the button at the centre
Medium to large **cover button** for each rosette

Pleated rosettes

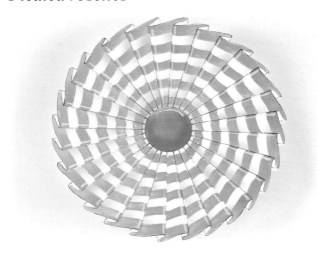

These are the most formal of the rosettes, with a sharply pleated ring of fabric centring on a covered button. The central button can be covered in the same fabric as the pleats or in a contrast: a particularly attractive effect is to use the same fabric as the furnishing for the button, with a contrast for the pleats, or to bind the pleated fabric and use the same binding to cover the button.

MAKING A PLEATED ROSETTE

1 Cutting out Draw a rough sketch of the finished rosette to get an idea of the size. Measure round the outside of the pattern to find the circumference, and cut a piece of fabric three times this measurement by the finished width of the whole rosette.

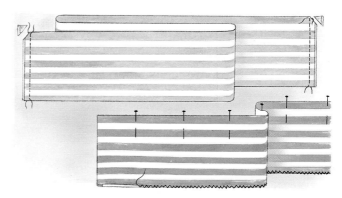

2 Preparing the fabric Fold the fabric in half, with right sides facing. Stitch along the two ends taking a 1cm (⅜in) seam allowance. Trim corners and turn right side out; press. Neaten the raw edges together with pinking shears and a row of straight stitching or with zigzag stitch. Insert pins along the folded edge at 2.5cm (1in) intervals or twice the width of each pleat, if different.

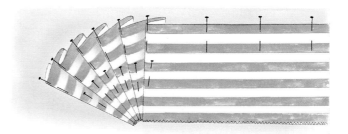

3 Pleating the fabric Pleat the fabric in a curve, with the neatened raw edges at the centre. Use the pins to mark the outer folds of the pleats, and pleat the fabric at the inside edge so tightly that there is only a small amount of fabric showing for each pleat. Finger press the pleats as you work and pin along the length of each one to hold.

Maltese cross rosette

This is a quick and easy alternative to the pleated rosette and is formed with either 2 or 3 bows superimposed and stitched together. It is usually made from one fabric, with a central button covered in the same or a contrasting fabric, however, for added interest the long edges of the loops can be bound with bias binding before the rosette is assembled. Cover the button in the main fabric or in the binding material.

MAKING A MALTESE CROSS ROSETTE

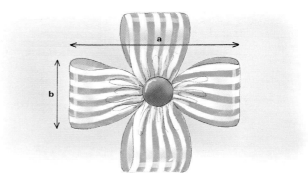

1 Cutting out Cut two or three strips of fabric (depending on the effect you require) twice the finished width of each loop (**a**) by twice the finished width of the rosette (**b**), adding 1cm (⅜in) seam allowances all round. Cut a circle of fabric for the covered button, and cover the button (follow the manufacturer's instructions).

2 Stitching the loops Fold the loops lengthways with right sides facing and pin and then stitch the long raw edges together, taking a 1cm (⅜in) seam allowance. Turn through to the right side, centre seam and press. Bind bias binding to the edges if desired. Neaten edges.

4 **Stitching the pleats** When you have finished the pleating, tuck the end of the fabric under the first pleat and pin. Hand stitch the pleats at the centre to hold using a double thread.

5 **Finishing off** Cover a button with fabric following the manufacturer's instructions. Working from the back of the rosette, stitch the fabric to the ring on the back of the button. Finally stitch the rosette in position on the soft furnishing.

tip

Ribbon rosette
Both the pleated and Maltese cross rosettes can be made with ribbon. You only need one layer of fabric instead of two and the edges of the ribbon do not require finishing, making the whole process quicker.

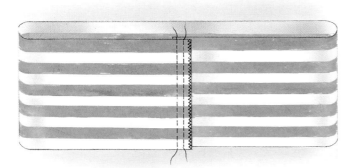

3 **Making the rosette** With the seam in the fabric uppermost, fold the ends of each loop to the centre so they overlap slightly in the middle, covering the seam. Run two rows of gathering stitches down the centre through all layers and gather up to give the loops their shape. Knot securely and add a further row of stitches to hold, if required. Cross the loops over each other at the centre, with the neatened fabric at the back; stitch securely to hold.

4 **Adding the covered button** Stitch the covered button to the centre of the rosette where the loops overlap. Finally stitch the rosette to the soft furnishing.

► **Versatile rosette**
A pretty double puff-ball rosette adds character to this petite bedroom chair. This isn't an item that most people would consider putting a rosette on, and it shows how versatile rosettes really are.

Puff-ball rosette

A puff-ball rosette has a voluptuous effect which works equally well in a grand, stately bedroom or a simple, Shaker style decor. Its shape encourages the play of light and shade, which makes it particularly effective with glossy fabrics like moiré, silk or satin, or with plain white linen or cotton.

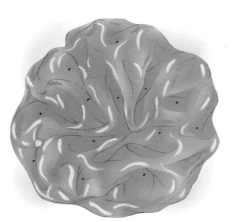

MAKING A PUFF-BALL

1 Cutting out Cut a circle of fabric 2-3 times the required width of the finished rosette: the larger the circle compared with the finished size, the more scrunched will be the finished rosette.

2 Gathering the rosette Thread a needle with a strong thread and knot the ends together to make a double thread. Run a row of running stitches round the circumference of the circle, 1.5cm (⅝in) from the edge, leaving the ends of the thread on the right side of the fabric. Pull up the thread to gather the raw edges into a small circle; knot to secure.

3 Making the rosette shape With a matching thread, take a small stitch in the centre of the rosette. Then, working from the right side, scrunch the fabric with one hand and stitch with the other, taking a small stitch in the hollows, about half way between the edge and the centre. This secures the fabric shape. If required, scrunch again and add further stitches until you are satisfied with the effect.

Window features

A crisp, white curtain with a lacy edging makes the freshest of window dressings. Bright sunlight filtered through the lace creates sun-bright patterns dancing on the wall or floor.

If you are making your own curtains, choose a crisp cotton, fresh linen or, for their easy-care properties, a fabric which includes a man-made fibre such as polyester. Select a boldly patterned and textured lace to go with these fabrics. A chunky cotton lace, crisp crochet edging, or swirling Battenburg lace all look good. Avoid complex curtain headings – a gently gathered fabric will allow the lace trim to show clearly.

Before making up the curtain wash both the fabric and the lace to prevent either shrinking more than the other after they have been sewn together.

The geometric design of many crochet or lace patterns complement coloured fabrics in formal patterns such as stripes, spots and checks, particularly if the background to the pattern is white to match the edging. The contrast between fabric and edging is eye-catching and unusual.

Alternatively, a ready-made tablecloth or dressing table runner with a lace edging or insert could be transformed into a simple flat curtain. Turn a casing at one end and hang it on a curtain wire or rod fixed at the window.

Nothing looks worse than slightly dingy white curtains at a window, so keep them fresh with regular washing – a final rinse in cold water starch before ironing will crisp the curtains and lace up beautifully.

▲ Hardanger embroidery
The edge of this flat curtain has been embroidered using the hardanger technique. Any even-weave fabric is suitable for this type of embroidery in which threads are removed after blocks of stitches have been worked, giving a lacy appearance to the finished cloth.

▲ Diamond lace insert
A ready-made table runner has found a new use as a modest curtain by simply turning a cased heading along one edge. The cotton fabric is less see through than a sheer or net, but not as heavy as a lined curtain. There are many types of lacy table runners which could be used.

▲ Edged with lace An old-fashioned lace edging with one shaped and one straight edge is ideal for adding interest to the leading edges of a lightweight pair of linen curtains.

▲ Austrian extravagance
The tape and cords which gather up this blind when raised are started a short way up from the lower edge. This allows a straight lace edging to be stitched to the edge of the blind.

◀ Crochet inserts and edges
Filet crochet can be bought by the yard or, if you are handy with a hook, made to measure. Turn narrow double hems along the panels before machine stitching the lace in position. The edging along the lower edge is added at the end.

Cupboard curtains

Glass-fronted cupboards, cabinets and bookcases are elegant additions to any room, enabling the contents to be seen and admired, while keeping them safe and free from dust. Books, ornaments and collections of small items look particularly attractive displayed behind glass, yet there are some occasions when you will want greater privacy, and here a curtain is ideal, casting a veil over the contents without obscuring the beauty of the glass doors.

Wardrobes, bathroom cupboards and cabinets with glass doors which are used for general storage, can all benefit from a lightweight curtain, which not only covers the contents but provides a decorative finish into the bargain. In bedrooms in particular, a curtain in a glass-fronted wardrobe has a soft and feminine look, with the richness of the grand country house style.

Unlike a standard net or sheer curtain, which is hung from the top, but left to hang freely at the bottom, a cabinet curtain is fixed at top and bottom, creating a more tailored, fitted shape. Since the curtain is held in this way, it is kept in place, even when the door is opened.

The fixed position of a cabinet curtain means that it can be used success-

▲ Fabric finish
A curtain in a fresh, flowery fabric is the perfect touch in this bathroom cabinet. The blue in the fabric echoes the blue lines on the cabinet mouldings, while the yellow enhances the warmth of the creamy paint.

fully not only on cupboard doors but also on larger room and house doors. On a door with a glass panel, it can be fitted on the inside, just covering the glass. On a door which is completely panelled with glass, as on french windows or patio doors, the curtain should be full length.

Fabric choices

Curtains for cupboards and cabinets can be made in any sheer, lacy, light or mediumweight woven fabric. The fabric can be generously gathered, or hung flat, like a blind. For preference, choose a fabric with a woven pattern, so that it is reversible, making it attractive from both sides.

Suitable fabrics include voile, broderie anglaise, net, cheesecloth, madras cotton, sprigged muslin, lining fabric or even fine silk. Sheer fabrics, such as muslin or voile look best when tightly gathered, while fabrics with large pictorial patterns or lace panels are often best displayed hung flat.

Curtain styles

Gathered curtain The fabric falls into soft folds, creating a very pretty, feminine style. Fine to mediumweight fabric is gathered on to a rod or plastic covered curtain wire at top and bottom. A small stand forms a frill. The fabric should be two to two and a half times the width of the rods to give sufficient fullness to the curtains.

Flat panel This is an ideal way of showing off a pretty lace panel, or an attractive piece of crochet or embroidery. It can be used when the fabric has a large pattern, or to display a stencilled design, painted on to an economical fabric like calico, and used to echo features in the room. Like a gathered curtain, a flat panel is fixed on two rods, but without fullness.

Hourglass curtain This attractive version of a gathered curtain adds interest to very plain, inexpensive fabrics such as muslin, voile or polyester cotton sheeting. The curtain is shaped on the top and bottom edges, and then gathered in with a ribbon at the centre to form the hourglass shape.

Materials

Two **curtain rods** or **curtain wires** for each curtain. On a wide curtain, wire may sag a little in the middle, so place it well above the glass so that the wire and casing do not show through the glass from the front.
Furnishing fabric.
Matching sewing thread.

GATHERED CABINET CURTAINS

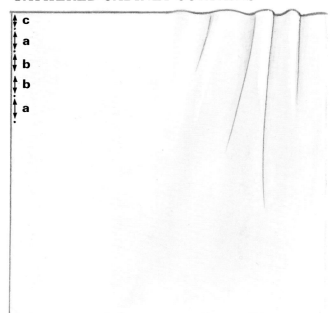

1 **The heading allowance** Although you can make these curtains with a simple cased heading they look more attractive with a stand. Measure the width of the rod or wire and add 5mm (¼in) for ease – this is the casing depth **(a)**. Decide on the depth of the stand, 3-5cm (1¼-2in) is usual **(b)**.

Add the casing and stand depths, multiply by two and add a 1cm (⅜in) seam allowance **(c)** for the total heading allowance.

2 **Cutting out** Position the rods or curtain wire inside the cupboard doors just above and below the glass; fix in place. Measure between the rods and add twice the heading allowance (for top and bottom) for the cut length. The cut width should be 2-2½ times the length of the rod. Cut and join pieces of the cut length using selvedges or with french seams (see page 93) to make a piece this width. Remember to match the pattern repeats.

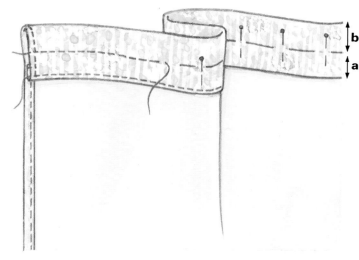

3 **Making the curtain** Turn under a double 1.5cm (⅝in) hem along each side edge of the curtain; pin and then stitch. At the top and bottom edges, turn under 1cm (⅜in) and then the depth of the casing **(a)** plus stand **(b)**, pinning and then stitching close to the inner fold.

4 **Making the casings** Measure from the stitching line towards the folded edge and mark a point the depth of the casing away from it **(a)**, using tailor's chalk. Draw a chalk line at this position at top and bottom edges, then pin and stitch along the chalk line.

5 **Finishing off** Lightly press the curtain, then slide a rod or curtain wire through each casing, gathering up the curtain as you do so. Fix in place at the door.

UNGATHERED CABINET CURTAIN

This is a simplified and economical version of the gathered cabinet curtain, and is usually made without a stand.

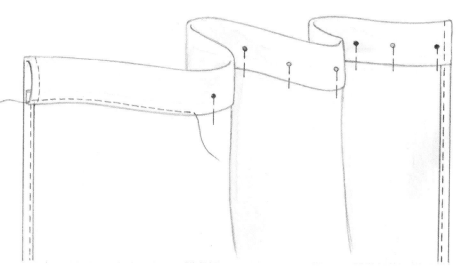

1 Cutting out Fix the two rods or curtain wires in place, and measure between them. If the rods or wires are no more than 1cm (⅜in) thick, the total cut length will be this measurement plus 8cm (3in). If the rods are thicker, measure the circumference and add 1.5cm (⅝in) for ease and turnings; double this and add to the measurement between the rods. For the cut width, measure the length of one rod and add 6cm (2½in) for side hem allowances, plus 5cm (2in) for ease.

2 Making the curtain Turn under 1.5cm (⅝in) double hems along both side edges; pin and then stitch. At the top and bottom edges, turn under 1cm (⅜in), then 3cm (1⅛in) or the depth of the casing, if deeper; pin and stitch close to the fold. Lightly press the curtain, then slide the rods into the casings.

◄ Lace panelling
The pattern on these lace curtains shows up beautifully when the fabric is hung, ungathered, behind the glass doors of the cabinet.

▼ Gathered curtain
Lightweight fabric falls into attractive, gentle folds when gathered on to rods in this hall cupboard, and when the door is closed, it hides the contents.

MAKING HOURGLASS CURTAINS

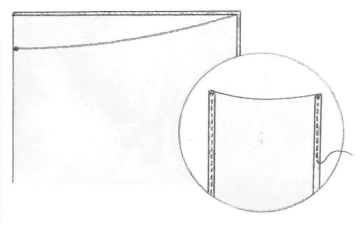

1 Cutting out Fix the curtain rods or wire at the glass door. Calculate the heading allowance as in step 1 for a gathered cabinet curtain. Measure from the top rod to the bottom one, pulling the tape measure inwards at the middle, as shown, then add twice the heading allowance for the cut length. Cut out fabric widths this long to make up a piece 2-2½ times the length of one rod. Join the fabric pieces together using the selvedges to prevent fraying or with french seams (see page 93). Make sure any pattern repeats match.

2 Making the curtain Fold the curtain in half lengthways with right sides together, to find the centre on the top and bottom edges. Mark a point at the centre, 7.5cm (3in) from the edge, then draw a gentle curve from this point to the corner, as shown, using tailor's chalk. Cut along the line at the top and bottom of the curtain. Stitch double 1.5cm (⅝in) side hems as in step 3 for a gathered cabinet curtain.

3 Finishing the curtain At the top edge, turn under 1cm (⅜in) and then the depth of the casing plus stand, pinning and then stitching in place close to the inner fold. Then complete the curtain, following steps 4 and 5 for a gathered cabinet curtain.

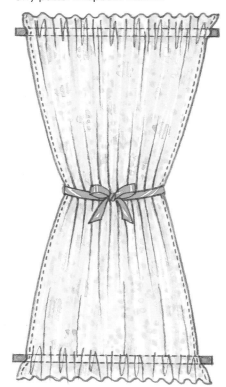

4 The final touch Hang the curtain and tie a length of wide ribbon round the centre of it to gather in the fabric; tie the ribbon in a bow.

▶ *Ivory elegance*
A strip of ivory fabric, used to tie back these elegant hourglass curtains, is topped with a pair of flamboyant rosettes made to match.

Shower curtains

The range of colours and patterns for ready-made plastic and vinyl curtains in the shops can be frustratingly limited, but if you have a particular style in mind for your country bathroom, making a shower curtain to fit in with the decor is probably the answer. A simple plastic curtain with eyelets for hanging is easy to make – adding a fabric outer curtain or a decorative drape makes it into something really special.

For a quick change, the gathered fabric curtain can be hung in front of the existing waterproof curtain so that the old curtain forms the lining of the new fabric one.

▼ Luxury curtain
A shower curtain made in furnishing fabric adds a luxurious touch to the bathroom. This one, using the same fabric as the Austrian blind, gives this bathroom a co-ordinated look. The simple stencil design, copied from the pattern of the fabric, completes the effect.

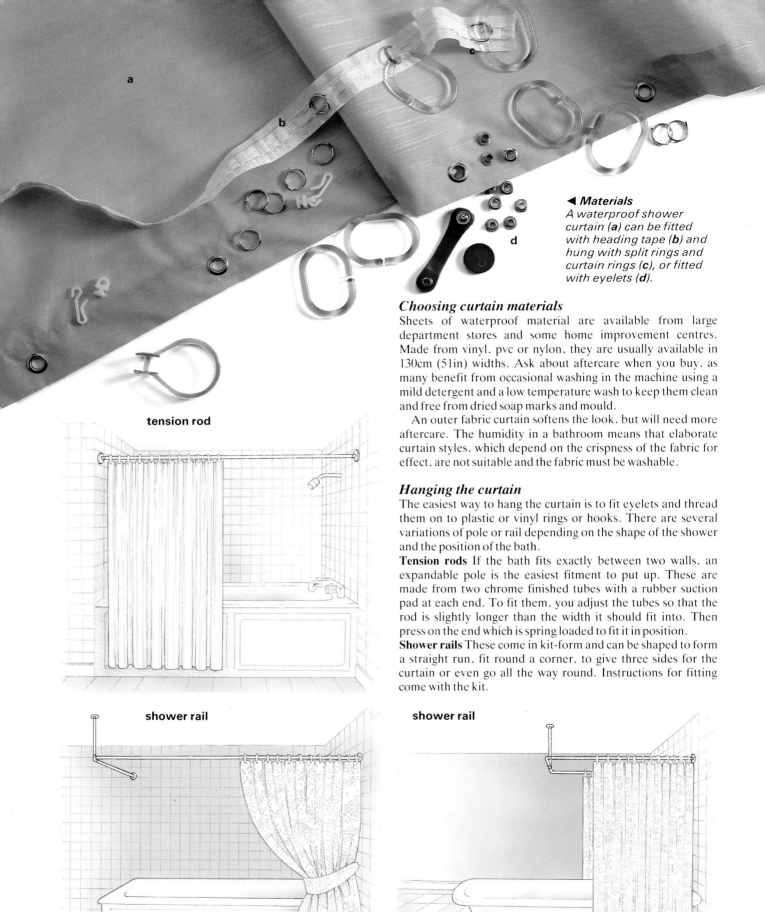

◀ **Materials**
*A waterproof shower
curtain (a) can be fitted
with heading tape (b) and
hung with split rings and
curtain rings (c), or fitted
with eyelets (d).*

Choosing curtain materials

Sheets of waterproof material are available from large
department stores and some home improvement centres.
Made from vinyl, pvc or nylon, they are usually available in
130cm (51in) widths. Ask about aftercare when you buy, as
many benefit from occasional washing in the machine using a
mild detergent and a low temperature wash to keep them clean
and free from dried soap marks and mould.

An outer fabric curtain softens the look, but will need more
aftercare. The humidity in a bathroom means that elaborate
curtain styles, which depend on the crispness of the fabric for
effect, are not suitable and the fabric must be washable.

Hanging the curtain

The easiest way to hang the curtain is to fit eyelets and thread
them on to plastic or vinyl rings or hooks. There are several
variations of pole or rail depending on the shape of the shower
and the position of the bath.

Tension rods If the bath fits exactly between two walls, an
expandable pole is the easiest fitment to put up. These are
made from two chrome finished tubes with a rubber suction
pad at each end. To fit them, you adjust the tubes so that the
rod is slightly longer than the width it should fit into. Then
press on the end which is spring loaded to fit it in position.

Shower rails These come in kit-form and can be shaped to form
a straight run, fit round a corner, to give three sides for the
curtain or even go all the way round. Instructions for fitting
come with the kit.

tension rod

shower rail

shower rail

Materials

Sheet vinyl, **nylon** or **plastic**
Nylon or polyester **thread**
Eyelet kit or eyelets and pliers
Chinagraph pencil
Shower curtain **rings** and **rail** or **rod**

WATERPROOF CURTAIN

1 Measuring up Measure the rail or pole for the curtain width and add 3cm (1¼in) to each side for double side hems. For a slight fullness, add up to a quarter of the width of the finished curtain. Measure from the rail or pole down to a point at least 20cm (8in) below the top of the bath or almost to the floor in a shower tray. Add 6cm (2½in) at top and bottom for hems.

2 Cutting out Cut out the waterproof fabric to make up a curtain to these measurements. Use french seams if you need to join widths. If the curtain is to be left without a fabric cover join widths so that the seam is centred or evenly spaced over the total width.

3 Hemming the edges Turn a double hem, 1.5cm (⅝in) and 1.5cm (⅝in) along each side. Do not use pins to hold – use paper clips, and machine stitch close to the fold using a wedge-pointed needle.

4 Hemming the top edge Turn a double hem, 3cm (1¼in) and 3cm (1¼in) along the top edge and machine stitch.

5 Positioning the eyelets Mark the top hem evenly 1cm (½in) down from the top edge at 15cm (6in) intervals. A chinagraph pencil is ideal for marking as it can be washed off with soapy water. Follow the instructions with the eyelet kit to make holes and insert eyelets.

6 Hanging the curtain Thread the rings on to the curtain rail and then hang the curtain on the rings, passing the break in the rings through the eyelets. Check the length of the curtain and turn up a double hem to finish.

LINED SHOWER CURTAIN

1 Measuring up Calculate the fabric requirements in the same way as for a waterproof shower curtain, adding extra if you plan to add a frill to the leading edge or a tieback to hold it back.

2 Making up Follow the instructions for a waterproof curtain to make two identical curtains, one in fabric and one in waterproof lining, each with eyelet holes along the top edge.

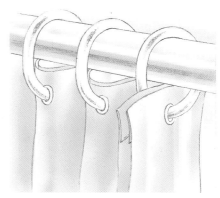

3 Hanging the curtains With the wrong sides of the fabrics together, pass the rings through both sets of eyelet holes to hang the curtains. When using the shower, the waterproof curtain hangs inside the bath with the fabric curtain outside.

tip

Instead of eyelets
If you do not have an eyelet kit, make vertical buttonholes, 5mm-1cm (¼-½in) long in the eyelet positions. Buy a ready-made plastic liner and hang the two curtains together.

DECORATIVE SHOWER CURTAINS

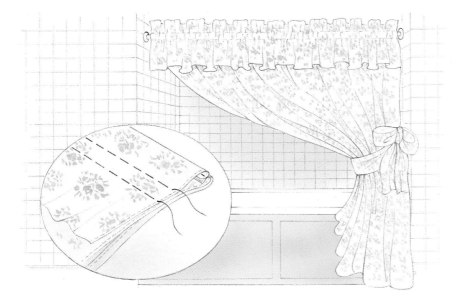

▲ **Frilled valance** A fixed curtain with a frilled valance, each 1½-2 times the width of the pole, has a really luxurious look. Hem the sides of the fabric curtain, lining and valance. Hem the lower edge of the valance. Place the valance and waterproof lining right sides together and then place the main fabric right side down on top of the valance with top edges matching; pin and stitch, then fold the lining to the back. Stitch a channel slightly wider than the pole through all three layers then hem the curtain and lining.

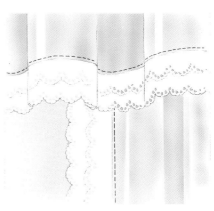

▲ **Lace trimming**
Add a pretty lace trim to the leading edge of a shower curtain to give it a country feel. If it has a valance, add the lace to the lower edge to complete the look. When sewing with plastic or vinyl fabrics, put a drop of sewing machine oil under the needle for smoother, easier stitching.

Shower curtains with decorative headings

A simple gathered or pencil pleat heading tape can be used for a fabric curtain to encourage the material to fall into soft folds. The outer curtain is made like a standard curtain from furnishing fabric and then combined with a waterproof lining with eyelet heading or existing shower curtain, hung wrong sides together round the shower or bath.

A gathered shower curtain can be hung from a shower rail, which has hooks like a standard curtain track, or from a pole. If the shower has a rail with hooks, gather up the outer curtain to fit the lining and then thread the hooks backwards through the tape before passing them through the corresponding eyelets of the waterproof lining. If the shower has a pole, thread split pins through the gathered tape and then slip these on to the rings on the pole with the eyelets of the lining. If the outer curtain sags slightly between hooks, additional hooks between eyelets will help to keep it straight.

◀ Lacy look
A lacy curtain, hung in front of the existing shower curtain, gives this shower a fresh, new look. Extra hooks on the gathered lace curtain, placed between the eyelets on the waterproof curtain, give the lace extra support.

▲ Tieback elegance
A long strip of spare fabric, sewn into a tube and then angled and neatened at both ends, makes a delightful tieback. The curtain is hung from a simple white tension rod rings and split rings.

Dressing table covers

A kidney-shaped dressing table, topped with a floral cotton cloth or a generously gathered sheer fabric, is a delightful addition to any bedroom, and an excellent place to display bedroom accessories such as a silver-plated brush and comb set or a jewellery box. The table underneath the cloth is often just an inexpensive piece of furniture made from pine or medium density fibreboard, so it is the cloth that really makes the table.

A new dressing table usually comes complete with the cover, and when the time comes to make a new one, this can be used as a pattern. However, to give the table a really fresh look, add some extra trimmings to the new cover, like fabric-covered piping round the top or binding round the hem. For a generously gathered, luxurious effect, make a frilly cover from a low-cost sheer fabric and finish each frill with a binding or braid trim to give it a chic, and expensive look.

Types of cover

The simplest type of dressing table cover has a flat, shaped top piece with a gathered, floor-length skirt attached, often with piping between the two pieces to define the shape. There is usually a shelf or cupboard in the table to provide hidden storage space for make-up and other bits and bobs, so it is necessary to have a split in the centre front of the cloth to allow for access.

Some dressing tables have a curtain rail running round the top for a floor-length skirt to run on. This makes it easy to draw back the cloth to get at the shelf

▼ Sheer sensation
A lavish, three-tiered dressing table cover made from layers of sheer fabric creates a romantic look which is ideal for this bedroom. Bobble braid on the lower edge of each frill provides definition.

or cupboard underneath. The rail is then hidden by a matching top cloth with a short, generously gathered frill, often with piping at the top of the frill and perhaps a matching binding trim round the lower edge as well.

If the dressing table does not have a curtain rail to hang the skirt from, a series of screw eyes can be put into the wood at intervals round the edge of the top for hanging. Again, this is then covered with a top cloth with short gathered frill. The long skirt can't be drawn back, but it can be pulled aside as required.

BASIC COVERS

1 Making a pattern Place a sheet of brown paper on top of the table and press it round the sides to mark the edge of the top. Cut out the paper, following the crease you have made, and then check the fit on the table. Alternatively, if there is an existing cover, unpick it and use this as a pattern.

2 Cutting out Cut out the top piece using your pattern, adding a 1.5cm (⅝in) seam allowance all round and making sure that large designs are centred. If using a fairly thin fabric, cut a second piece from fusible interfacing and fuse to the wrong side for added body.

For the skirt, measure the drop from the top of the table to the floor; add 3cm (1¼in) for a hem and 1.5cm (⅝in) for a seam allowance. Cut lengths of fabric this measurement which when joined, selvedge to selvedge, will make up a piece 1½-2 times the measurement round the table-top.

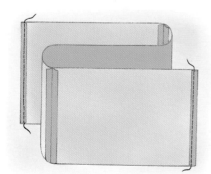

3 Making the skirt Pin and then stitch the skirt pieces together to make one piece. Press seam allowances open. Turn and pin a double 1.5cm (⅝in) hem at each end; stitch.

4 Hemming the skirt Turn and pin a double 1.5cm (⅝in) hem along the lower edge of the fabric. Stitch by hand or machine.

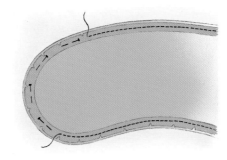
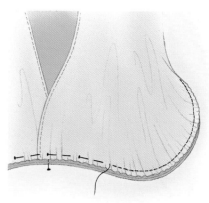

5 Piping the top If required, make up enough bias binding to go round the top piece, plus 2.5cm (1in) for an overlap. Cover piping cord in the bias binding and pin to the seamline of the top piece, snipping into the binding fabric for ease at the curves; stitch.

6 Gathering the skirt Fold the skirt in half, end to end, and mark the middle of the fabric with a pin or tailor's chalk. Run two rows of gathering stitches along the top of the skirt 1cm (⅜in) and 2cm (¾in) from the raw edge, stopping and starting at the mark.

7 Attaching the skirt Mark the centre front and centre back of the top piece with pins. Pin one end of the skirt piece to the centre front of the top, with right sides facing; pin the skirt to the centre back with marks matching, then overlap the remaining end with the first end by 8cm (3in) and pin. Pull up the gathering stitches until the skirt fits the top. Arrange the gathers evenly, then tack and remove the pins; stitch, taking a 1.5cm (⅝in) seam allowance.

8 Finishing off Remove the tacking stitches and neaten the seam allowances with zigzag. Press the cloth lightly before positioning it on the table.

▼ *Slimline cover*
The crisp furnishing fabric used to make this basic dressing table cover with piped top creates an elegant, slimline effect.

THREE-TIERED COVER

A three-tiered dressing table cover is a variation of the basic cover which looks particularly attractive with sheer or fine fabrics since the style creates extra volume.

1 Cutting out Cut out the top piece as in steps 1-2 for a basic dressing table cover. Measure up and make the skirt in the same way as in step 2 left, but instead of making it 1½-2 times the measurement round the table, make it only the same measurement as the table, adding 4cm (1½in) for side hems and 8cm (3in) for an overlap.

Cut and join strips of fabric to make up three frills 2-3 times the width of the skirt. Each frill should be a third of the finished skirt drop plus 4.5cm (1¾in) for hem and seam allowances; to two of the frills add 5cm (2in) for an overlap.

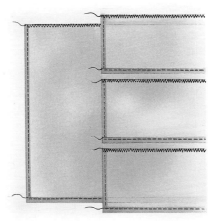

2 Preparing the skirt pieces Turn and pin a double 1.5cm (⅝in) hem at each end of each frill and each end of the skirt; stitch. Turn and pin a double 1.5cm (⅝in) hem along the lower edge of each piece; stitch. Neaten the top edge of each frill with zigzag or overlock. If required, stitch braid on the right side over the hems of the three frills.

3 Gathering the frills Divide and mark each frill into four. Run two rows of gathering stitches 1cm (⅜in) and 2cm (¾in) from the neatened edge of each frill, stopping and starting at marks.

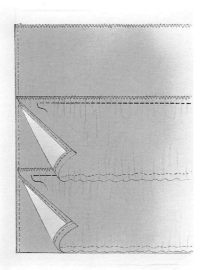

4 Attaching the frills Mark the skirt into four equal sections. Gather up the two deeper frills to fit the skirt, matching marks. Pin the first one to the skirt with hem edges level and right sides up; tack and then stitch 1.5cm (⅝in) from the neatened edge, between the gathering rows. Pin the other frill above the first so that it overlaps it by 5cm (2in); tack and stitch.

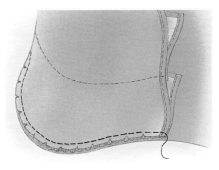

5 Completing the cover Gather up the remaining frill and tack to the top piece with raw edges level and right sides facing; overlap the ends of the frill by 8cm (3in) at the front. Pin the skirt face down on top, with the ends overlapping in the same place as the frill – snip into the seam allowances at the corners for ease. Tack, remove pins and then stitch taking a 1.5cm (⅝in) seam allowance. Remove all tacking and gathering stitches and lightly press the cloth before positioning it on the table.

Protecting the top
A sheer or lightweight fabric may not cover up the fibreboard table-top, so slip a piece of neatened lining fabric, cut to the same size, underneath the cloth. To protect the table from knocks and spills, have some protective glass cut to fit and put this on top.

TWO-PIECE COVER

Kidney-shaped dressing tables which have a track running round the edge of the top, have a two-piece cover – a skirt, hanging from the track and a top piece over the table-top which also covers the track. The skirt can also be hung with Velcro or with a series of screws and eyelets.

Standard curtain tape, stitched to the top of the skirt, ensures that the fabric is evenly gathered.

1 Cutting out the skirt Measure the drop from the track to the floor and add 8cm (3¼in) for the heading and hem. Cut lengths of fabric this measurement, which when joined, will make up a piece 1½-2½ times the measurement round the table-top – use 1½ times the measurement for standard fabrics and up to 2½ times for fine fabrics.

▼ Binding trim
The wide blue binding round the lower edge of the frill emphasizes the shape of this two-piece cover.

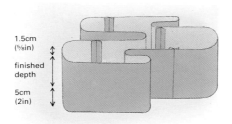

1.5cm (⅝in)

finished depth

5cm (2in)

2 Cutting out the top Make a pattern for the top as in step 1 for a basic dressing table cover. For the top frill cut and join strips of fabric to make up a loop 1½-2½ times the measurement round the table-top; press seams open. The strips should be the depth of the finished frill – 10-15cm (4-6in) is ideal – plus 3cm (1¼in) for a hem and 1.5cm (⅝in) for a seam allowance. If binding the lower edge, omit the hem allowance.

3 Joining the skirt Pin and then stitch the fabric pieces for the skirt together, selvedge to selvedge, to make one large piece. Turn and pin a double 1.5cm (⅝in) side hem at each end; stitch.

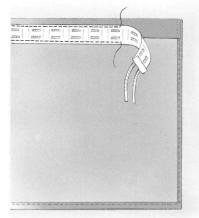

4 Making the skirt Turn a double 1.5cm (⅝in) hem along the lower edge of the skirt; pin and then stitch. Turn 5cm (2in) to the wrong side along the top edge and pin standard heading tape on top. Stitch in place along each edge of the tape (see page 93).

5 Hanging the skirt Gather up the skirt by pulling up the heading tape and attach to the curtain track with curtain hooks. If the table doesn't have a curtain track round it, a series of screw eyes can be fixed at 15cm (6in) intervals round the table-top. Slip curtain hooks into the gathered heading tape and slip them through the screw eyes to hang.

6 Making the top frill Pin and stitch a double 2.5cm (1in) hem on the lower edge of the frill. Divide the frill into four equal sections and mark. Run two rows of gathering stitches 1cm (⅜in) and 2cm (¾in) from the top edge, stopping and starting at marks.

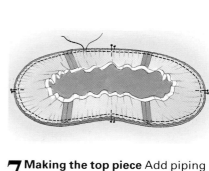

7 Making the top piece Add piping to the top piece, if required, as in step 5 for a basic cover. Divide the top into four equal sections, and gather up the frill to fit as in steps 5-7 for a basic cover, matching marks. Tack and then stitch the frill to the top, with right sides facing and the piping sandwiched in between, taking a 1.5cm (⅝in) seam allowance. Remove the tacking and gathering stitches, press top piece and then arrange it on the table, covering the track.

BASIC TECHNIQUES

MAKING BIAS BINDING

Bias binding protects raw edges and also provides a firm decorative finish. It comes in ready-prepared form in a wide range of colours and in several different widths. For a really personal finishing touch, make your own bias binding from a matching or contrasting fabric in exactly the width you want.

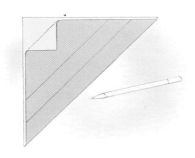

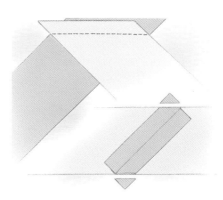

1 Fabric quantities For the width of the binding, allow an extra 2.5cm (1in) for seam allowances. For the length, allow an extra 2cm (¾in) for joining.

2 Cutting the bias strips Fold the fabric diagonally, so the cut edge lies along the selvedge. With your hand flat against the fabric fold, cut along the fold. Both diagonal edges are now cut along the fabric bias. Mark the required strip widths along the diagonal edges and cut out.

3 Joining strips together Fabric strips must be joined together on the straight grain. Place strips with right sides together; pin and stitch with a 6mm (¼in) seam allowance. Press seam open. Trim off points

---

BINDING EDGES

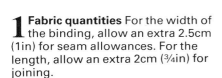

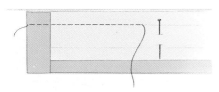

1 Pin and stitch Turn in 1.5cm (⅝in) at one end of the binding. Starting at this end, place one long raw edge of the bias binding to the raw edge of the fabric, right sides together. Pin and stitch, following the first fold in the binding.

2 Finishing off Fold the binding over to the wrong side so that the centre fold in the binding is level with the edge of the fabric. Tuck the other edge of the binding under along the last fold and hand stitch to the fabric to complete.

POSITIONING CURTAIN TAPE

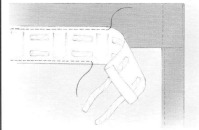

1 Positioning the heading tape Turn down the top edge for the width of the tape, plus the depth of the stand heading. Position the heading tape to the wrong side of the fabric, with base edge just covering the raw fabric edge; pin.

SEWING FRENCH SEAMS

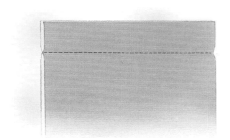

1 With wrong sides together, machine 5mm (³⁄₁₆in) from the seamline, within the seam allowance.

2 Press seam open and trim both raw edges to 3mm (⅛in).

3 Fold along machine line with right sides together. Tack and machine on seamline. Press seam to one side.

TAPING A LAMPSHADE FRAME

The frame must be taped first if the shade is to be fixed to it. Using strong cotton tape (not bias binding) start by taping the struts and then tape the top and bottom ring. If you want the tape to match the shade, dye it first. Measure each strut and round each ring and multiply by three to give the total length of tape needed.

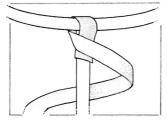

1 Starting to tape Cut a piece of tape three times the length of the strut. Starting at the top front of one strut, wind the end over the top ring, round behind and across to wrap over the loose end to secure.

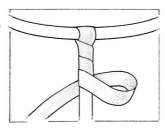

2 Taping the strut Work down the strut, wrapping the tape diagonally, so that each wrap of the tape just overlaps the previous one. Pull the tape very tightly as you wrap – once taping is complete it must not move on the strut.

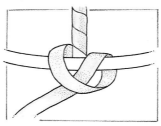

3 Fixing the end When you reach the bottom ring, pass the tape round the ring and back through the last loop to make a knot. Pull tight and leave the loose end of tape dangling for the time being. Tape each strut except one.

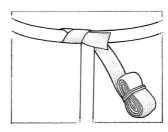

4 Taping the ring Measure the top ring, the bottom ring and the last untaped strut and cut a piece of tape three times this length. Wind up tape and secure it with an elastic band leaving about 20cm (8in) to work with. Start taping the top ring at the join with the untaped strut. Hold the end of the tape against the ring then wind it to the inside and back over the ring, catching the loose end under it. Work round the top ring as on the struts.

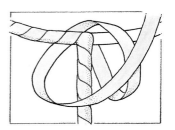

5 A figure of eight When you reach the join between each strut and top ring, wind the tape round the stut and ring in a figure of eight. When you arrive back at the untaped strut wind round this in a figure of eight and then tape down the strut. At the bottom of the strut, wind round it and the ring in a figure of eight and continue to tape the bottom ring in the same way as the top. When you reach each strut, trim off the surplus tape leaving 1cm (⅜in) and work a figure of eight over it to secure.

6 Finishing off Trim off any surplus tape to leave 6mm (¼in). Turn under end and hand stitch to hold.

Index

Page numbers in *italic* refer to picture captions

Acknowledgements

Photographers: Araidne Holland 7, 15-18, 43, 59, 67, 70, 72, 74, 79; Elizabeth Bradley Designs Ltd 63; Boys Syndication 78(r), 80(tl); Cy De Cosse 65-66, 84; Dorma 48(t); Dovedale Fabrics 90-91; Eaglemoss Publications Ltd (Simon Page-Ritchie) 1, 11-14, 23, 26-28, 31-34, (John Suett) 35, 37-39, 41-42, 49-50, 53-54, 77-78(l), (Steve Tanner) 8-10, 25, 29-30, 44, 46(b), 51-52, 55, 57-58, 86, 88(l); Anna French Ltd 71, 73; Liberty 46(t); Modes et Travaux 19-21, 48(br), 60, 62(b), 64(bl); Mondadori Press (Nocentini/Frateschi) 89; Richard Paul 3, 48(bl), 64(br), 69, 83; Rufflette 88(r); Serail Carre 62(t); Smallbone of Devizes 81; B & R Stoeltie 45; VPM Redaktionsservice 80(tr), (c), (b); EWA (Michael Dunne) 64(t), (Andreas von Einsiedel) 75, (Di Lewis) 47, (Neil Lorimer) 62(c), (Spike Powell) 92.
Illustrators: Julie-Ann Burt 68(bl), 83(b); Terry Evans 12-14, 24-26, 28, 32-34, 40-42, 50, 82, 83(t), 84; Garden Studios (Sally Holmes) 54, (Liz Pepperell) 20-22; Will Giles & Sarah Pond 93; Christine Hart-Davies 30, 68(t), 69(r), 70(br); John Hutchinson 7-10, 16-18, 36-38, 44-46, 52, 56-58, 60-61, 72-74, 76-78, 86-87, 90-92.